TRAILS Among the COLUMBINE

A Colorado High Country Anthology

SUNDANCE
Books

Editor's Preface

Before you lies a book, and an adventure. The volume you hold in your hands, **Trails Among The Columbine 1986**, continues in the tradition of Sundance's scenic calendars and previous volume of the same name. It is an exploration in words and photographs of the magnificent Colorado high country.

Previous calendars, and last year's volume traversed the state, revealing scenic beauty, history and adventure throughout Colorado. This year's volume focuses on an area for which those of us at Sundance have a special fondness: the San Juan Mountain region of southwestern Colorado.

Many of our readers have a special interest in narrow-gauge railroads and their history; perhaps nowhere in the world is there a place more special to narrow-gauge enthusiasts, or railroad history fans in general, than the San Juans. For many, the narrow-gauge capital of the world is Silverton, deep in the heart of the San Juans. This, and Silverton's incredible natural beauty, led Sundance to spend seven wonderful years with its offices and production facilities housed in the historic Rio Grande depot there. Even though Sundance now finds itself in Denver, Silverton and the San Juans continue to occupy a very special and prominent place in our hearts. Some of us (your editor, for example) still call it home!

Just what is it that brings visitors from all corners of the globe to the San Juans? Why would your editor consider it better to commute 750 miles, round trip, to and from work in Denver, than to leave this magical place? Perhaps the stories and photographs before you will help to provide an answer.

Hopefully those of you who know the San Juans will find this book a wonderful evocation of fond memories, and those who have yet to discover the San Juans in person will find this book a marvelous prelude to something even better than stories and photos: a personal visit to what many, myself included, consider to be the most beautiful corner of God's green earth.

One last word. The photographs and stories in this book have been prepared, not by journalists from afar, sent on assignment, but by those who have lived here, or nearby for many years. It is a book about a special place, by people who know it, and love it. These people are as special as the place itself. I know you will enjoy their images and recollections.

Steven J. Meyers, Editor

FRONT COVER: Durango & Silverton Narrow Gauge Railroad locomotive Number 497, rebuilt from a standard-gauge locomotive, is shown making the final curve into Silverton loaded with passengers re-living the "Old West." Dell A. McCoy Photograph

BACK COVER: The morning sun, rising from behind Kendall Mountain, will evaporate the mist rising from the hillsides surrounding Silverton. Dell A. McCoy Photograph

Trails Among The Columbine
A Colorado High Country Anthology

250 Broadway, Denver, Colorado 80203

Published by
Sundance Publications, Ltd., Denver, Colorado

Graphical Presentation and Printing by
Sundance Publications, Ltd., Denver, Colorado

Binding by
Hawley Bookbinding Co., Denver, Colorado

Typesetting by
The Silverton Standard and The Miner
Silverton, Colorado

Editor - Steven J. Meyers
Production Manager - Dell A. McCoy

ISBN 0-913582-43-3

TABLE OF CONTENTS

Colorado Columbine

The official state flower of Colorado, the Blue Columbine, photographed as it was found, basking in the sunshine near Animas Forks, a few miles above Silverton.

The Colorado Blue Columbine was adopted the official state flower of Colorado in 1899. It belongs to the Ranunculus or buttercup family. The lovely, long-spurred, nodding blossoms are Colorado sky blue with a snow white cup reminiscent of the champagne powder on the state's ski slopes. A profusion of yellow anthers recalls Colorado's gold rush days. In their natural state, Columbines are found in moist, shady places from the lower foothills to just above timberline, but they seem to be most beautiful in aspen groves around 8,000 feet in elevation.

5

Fly Fishing

*A*bout ten in the morning I decided that I'd had enough of darkroom chemicals, halftone negatives and stale air. I'd begun working at seven that morning, and planned to work fairly late into the night. Although I couldn't see through the opaque, windowless walls, I knew that another glorious San Juan autumn day lay six inches away through the dry wall, two by four studs, fiberglass insulation, sheathing, and lap siding of the old Denver and Rio Grande depot in which I worked. The warm sun, blue sky and quaking golden aspen were out there and I knew it. These I have enough difficulty resisting, but the rushing waters of Lime Creek, filled with trout, were also out there, and that was just too much. It was time for an extended break. I finished what I was doing, shut down my equipment, and left the darkroom. Outside my car was waiting. It had been equipped for fishing, and used for little else for weeks. In the trunk were waders which scarcely had time to dry between outings, enough fly rods, reels and lines to equip a small boy scout troop, more flies, leaders and paraphernalia than anyone could use in a lifetime. More and more, life seemed to revolve around trout, and trying to fool them with feathers and fur tied to a hook; more and more, the physical accoutrements of my life began to reflect this wonderful obsession. My car was no exception. In it, surrounded by tackle, I drove down the dirt road which parallels Lime Creek, freed from the drudgery of indoor work, filled with the expectation of sun on my skin, fresh air in my lungs, clear water tugging at my legs and wild trout tugging on my line.

For a little over a month that autumn it was my regular routine to work in the morning, fish from ten until around three or four in the afternoon, and then return to the darkroom for an evening of still air, darkness, chemicals and photographic procedures. During that month I fished many miles of Lime Creek, caught hundreds of trout, observed many more, and learned how profound my ignorance of their habitat and habits had been; even more important were the discoveries I made about myself and my place in the natural world. In that month I fished more hours than I have been able to fish in some entire seasons, and during the vast majority of those hours I had this magnificent trout stream entirely to myself. Rarely did I see another angler. I did not have to drive all day to find beauty, a stream or fish. Fifteen minutes in the car was enough (I

Deceived by a Thunder Creek Streamer, a fat, wild brook trout lies in the grass beside the beaver pond where it was taken.

The San Juans
by Steven J. Meyers

After a successful evening spent fishing the waters of Little Molas Lake above Silverton, a happy angler prepares to clean his catch. This lovely lake, accessible by automobile a short distance from U.S. Highway 550 at Molas Pass, provides excellent fishing and extraordinary scenery.

could have walked to good fishing as well, but Lime Creek was my obsession that fall, and it was a few more miles from home than Mineral Creek which I can see from my bedroom window). Where else, I wondered, could such a blissful state exist? Where else, indeed, but the San Juans.

Obsession. I've used the word twice. For those familiar with flyfishing or its literature the use of the word comes as no surprise. For others it might seem a bit extreme. After all, who can take this sport so seriously that it becomes an obsession? Who could possibly get excited about dangling a hook in the water and waiting for a fish to stupidly ingest it? Fishing might well be the most boring pastime in existence. Doctors routinely prescribe fishing as an antidote to stress. Can a stress antidote be obsessive? Those of us who share this magnificent obsession are chuckling silently. No matter what the rest of the world thinks of fishing, we know that flyfishing in general, and flyfishing for trout in particular, have an incredible potential for neurotic addiction, that the fishing isn't the half of it, and that if God had intended that flyfishing for trout should be an antidote to stress, a blissful and mild pastime, a sport which created lowered heartbeats and blood pressure, He never would have devised large old trout with picky appetites who rise to within microns of our flies only to turn slowly away in disgust, or deep bodied rainbow trout who take flies only when they are tied to nearly invisible gossamer threads which seem to break when you look at them, who flee leaping and rolling with the current leaving your line shattered along with your hopes, your heart pounding in excitement and confusion.

The obsession begins, as most obsessions do, innocently enough. We often fish as children. With bait. With lures. Sometimes we are introduced to flyfishing by our fathers who fish ahead of us gracefully casting the flowing fly line. Sometimes we learn from our grandfathers, or a friend who is older, that there is a deeper joy in fishing than hauling out fish who have swallowed worms deep into their gullets and who must be killed, whether we would eat them or not, because our hooks have been taken so deeply. Often flyfishing begins with the love and respect we have for another, an outdoorsman we know who is at home in the woods and says with clarity and conviction, "given a choice I would fish the fly." Occasionally the obsession begins with envy. Sometimes those wielders of the flylines and feathered offerings fish circles around us, and always, it would seem, they do so with more grace and elegance.

9

Adams, Dry Fly

We learn to cast the flyline by practicing on grass or still ponds. We are taught by our fathers, grandfathers and companions in the woods. Soon we learn that knowing how to cast is not enough. We must know to whom we cast, and on what they feed. We begin to learn about the trout, and this we learn best from the trout themselves. They tell us what they will eat when, where they want it, and how they want it to look. They tell us this by taking our flies, or rejecting them. We begin to be concerned with trout biology, and this leads directly to trout ecology, the study of their habitat. We learn about the things they eat, mostly insects, and the places they live. Often we begin to tie our own flies (how can some shop in Montana know what a Lime Creek caddis fly looks like?). We begin to read the voluminous literature which flyfishing has generated. We learn of trouting's history, and come to appreciate the development of our equipment, the transition from horsehair to silk, and then to synthetic lines; from solid wood, to split bamboo, to steel, fiberglass and carbon fiber rods. We begin to see and understand subtlety and nuance in various trout, in different streams, in casts, in flies, in the woods which contain the streams, in a world which contains anglers and salmonids...on and on it goes, without end. What is this, but obsession? Fortunately, it's also a hell of a lot of fun; otherwise, we'd all have to be committed!

For the obsessive flyfisherman (or anyone else, for that matter), there are few pleasures to rival finding oneself in the San Juans. The sheer number of trout filled streams, lakes and ponds is staggering. The beauty of the region in which these streams flow, in which the lakes and ponds sit, beyond description. To be here fishing is to be considerably more than just happy.

Other areas have more productive streams in terms of the numbers of fish and their size. This is certainly the case on some of America's more famous trout streams. Unfortunately, these streams also often have more human biomass as well (usually clad in waders and standing knee deep in the pool you wanted to fish). The trout in some streams are more difficult to catch than the average San Juan trout. A Letort River brown trout in central Pennsylvania will be significantly harder to fool than most of the trout you see in the San Juans, and anglers looking for educated trout would do better to look to such streams for this kind of challenge. San Juan trout are rarely selective, that is, they usually will eat more than one kind of food at a given time, and therefore can be taken on a wide variety of appropriate flies. You will find that fishing the San Juans will yield little in the way of bragging rights about catching ultra-smart or ultra-selective trout. What the obsessive and the neophyte angler both experience in the San Juans is the joy of fishing in solitude, surrounded by great natural beauty for something which is more precious than gold, and perhaps more rare: wild, stream bred trout. For me no angling pleasure rivals that of taking a brilliantly colored, genetically pure wild cutthroat trout from a high headwater stream. This trout is to a cross-bred or hatchery reared trout what grandma's fried chicken is to chicken nuggets. Sadly, most of America's streams are filled with chicken nuggets. San Juan trout, especially those from the high streams, are one's you would be proud to share with grandma.

Grey Hackle Peacock, Dry Fly

Steven J. Meyers Photograph

Elk-hair Caddis, Dry Fly

I have fished for educated brown trout in the limestone streams of central Pennsylvania, and I must admit that catching trout there was a very pleasant and rewarding experience. Still, there is something which disturbs me about a trout who continues to feed when humans are about thrashing the water with fat fly lines, fish who move away, sometimes, but who seem to trust that their knowledge of flies and hooks and leaders will protect them from man. San Juan trout run from man at the slightest indication of his presence. They remind us of our true genetic heritage as hunters and predators. We are, without question, the most dangerous creature in the woods. Those educated trout may know the difference between a thorax-tied mayfly dun, and a no-hackle dun, but they seem to have lost their fear of man. Which trout is truly smarter?

Having said that San Juan trout are not particularly selective regarding food might lead one to believe that any old fly tied onto a leader will result in fish. This is not the case. Here, as elsewhere, some flies are more appropriate at certain times than others, and nearly always a fly which imitates a predominant food form will out catch a fly which the trout do not expect to see. Broadly suggestive flies seem to do better than highly specific imitations. If I were pressed for a recommendation based on my own experience, I would have to answer that there are two flies without which I would feel naked in the San Juans. These are the Elk Hair Caddis dry fly, and the Gold-ribbed Hares Ear nymph. A newcomer to the area would do well fishing these in various sizes until he or she developed personal preferences based on specific experiences.

In the streams, I have rarely encountered anything approximating selective feeding, and in trout I have taken on dry flies, I have almost always found an astounding variety of foods. Oddly, I have found few adult caddis flies in the stomachs of fish I have examined. More often I find a bizarre mixture of terrestrial insects (bees, wasps, ants, etc.) and assorted aquatic insects, both adults and underwater forms. The success of the Elk Hair Caddis lies, I think, more in its behavior on the water, than in any preference the trout might have for adult caddis flies. It is an appropriate fly (caddis flies are fairly common), but more important than that is the fact that it floats well in the often turbulent water of high altitude freestone streams, it floats with its body low in the water attracting attention from the fish, and it is easy to see, keeping the angler from missing fish due to undetected strikes. For comparison, consider the ant which is almost always found in stomach autopsies, but which rarely catches fish for me, except in extremely slow and still water. Ants are just too hard to see in the average mountain stream. A white wing helps the visibility problem, but they still don't seem to catch fish as well as the caddis. If I had only one dry fly, it would be the caddis.

The Gold-ribbed Hare's Ear nymph is successful largely because of its ability to suggest a wide range of underwater insect forms, the unique and effective appearance that its scraggly body presents in the water, and the sparkle (presumed to resemble air bubbles which often appear on the bodies of natural insects like emerging caddis flies) of the gold ribbing. Both the Elk Hair Caddis and the Gold-ribbed Hare's Ear are readily available in tackle shops.

Steven J. Meyers Photograph

Brown Bi-visible, Dry Fly

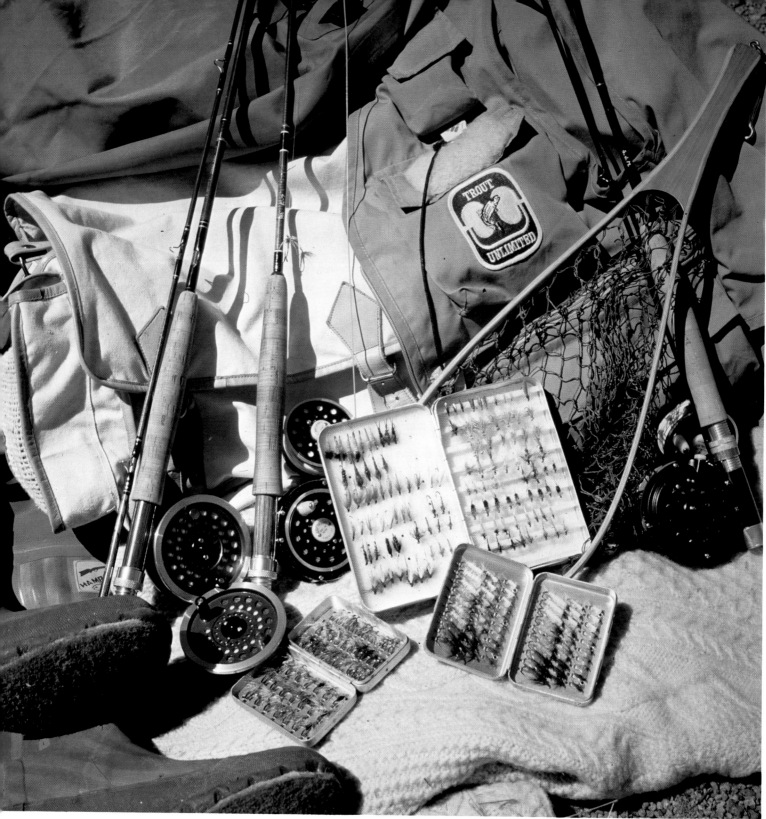

Steven J. Meyers Photograph

Modern fly fishing tackle—consisting of graphite rods, lightweight reels with adjustable drag, floating lines which actually float, sinking lines which predictably and dependably sink, vests which neatly organize equipment, leaders with both strength and delicacy, waders that keep the angler dry, and fly patterns which, over the years, have evolved to include some of considerable sophistication—is a far cry from the tackle of our grandfathers. The fundamental skills, and pleasures, of flyfishing, however, have changed little in centuries.

Another favorite fly for the San Juans is the Bi-visible dry fly. This fly consists of hackle wound the length of the fly hook, with several turns of white hackle wound near the head of the fly. My favorites are the Brown Bi-visible (brown hackle with white near the head) and Badger Bi-visible (badger hackle with white near the head). Once again, the main advantage would appear to be the fly's behavior on the water (it floats like a cork) and high visibility to the angler. This fly does well drifted with the current, and also skated or twitched. It moves over the water when skated, not in the water, and appears to behave like a hovering insect. Often this movement of the fly will encourage strikes from reluctant fish.

A final all purpose, do everything kind of dry fly which I would not leave at home is the Royal Wulff. Just what it is that makes fish strike the Royal Wulff or any of the other permutations of the popular Royal Coachman is not known. Some have argued that it resembles, in shape, an ant. Perhaps, but I haven't seen too many ants with color as gaudy as this. Whatever the source of its effectiveness, there is no doubt that it works. The Wulff version, with its white hair wing and deer hair tail floats extremely well, is highly visible, and is well suited to the riffles and rapids of headwaters fishing.

One last all purpose dry fly which needs mention is the Adams. It is, perhaps more than any other, the universal dry fly. It imitates many mayflies well, has been called a caddis imitation (although it would have to be tied with its wing down along the back, and therefore no longer be a true Adams as far as I'm concerned, in order to qualify as a caddis imitation in my book), and matches, in its generally dull coloration and subtly mixed hackle/wing hues, a great many insects who hang around trout waters.

There are other dry flies that I use, especially if I find fish taking a particular insect, or see evidence of one on the water in abundance. These include the grasshopper, some specific mayfly patterns, stonefly patterns, Wulff variations, midge imitations, beetles and large diptera imitations like the Gray-hackle Peacock which seems to work well when there are deer flies about. The list could continue. In general, when I fish fast flowing streams, I choose flies for their ability to float and be seen. When the water slows down, giving both the fish and myself a better look, I switch to patterns that imitate more directly the insects I think the trout are taking.

Diminutive, but precious, a true Colorado native, the wild cutthroat trout becomes more and more difficult to find in its pure form. This stream-bred native waits on a streamside rock for reviving and release into the clear high altitude stream from which he was removed.

Ted's Stonefly, Nymph

Wet flies and nymphs generally do better, when fished carefully, than dry flies. This makes sense. Trout are variously estimated to take from seventy-five to ninety percent of their food beneath the surface. Contrary to popular opinion, it is more difficult to fish a wet fly well than a dry fly. Talk to anyone who has been fishing for a long time, and ask them what they think the single most difficult technique is, and I bet you they'll answer fishing the nymph dead drift, upstream. Some have gone so far as to call this particular act the one which separates advanced fisherman from average fisherman. I love the rise of a trout to a dry fly, but I would have to agree that fishing the wet fly and nymph well requires an extraordinary amount of practice and skill, and that doing it well is extremely satisfying. Once learned, the rewards are tremendous.

I have already mentioned the Gold-ribbed Hare's Ear. It is, without question, the closest thing we have to a universal wet fly/nymph. In various sizes, and fished in various ways, it can be used to imitate everything from emerging caddis pupae to stone fly nymphs tumbling in the turbulent currents of rapids. It is the one nymph to have when you have only one. But what fisherman wants to have only one? More specific stonefly nymph imitations like the Montana Nymph and Woolly Worm do well in waters where stoneflies are found (usually just downstream of rapids, and in rocky riffles). Traditional wet flies (now largely unfashionable, having been replaced in many fisherman's minds and fly boxes by the more directly imitative nymphs) do extremely well in the streams of the San Juans. Their ability to suggest a

wide variety of insects, from drowned terrestrials to true nymphs, to winged swimming underwater adults (as recently suggested by Georges Odier of Aspen) is unrivaled. There is no question in my mind that they ought to be fished, and fished often. The Western Coachman and the Rio Grande King, two similar flies, are quite popular and successful. Wet Light and Dark Cahills are often seen on the leaders of old timers who will astound you with the numbers of fish they take. Traditional streamers and bucktails work well in deep pools. Lately I have taken to soft hackled wet flies, perhaps the most ancient of flies still fished, and pretty much gone from the scene in this country until revived by Sylvester Nemes of Chicago. Besides being among the most simple and elegant flies, they are a joy to fish, and extraordinarily effective. These flies can be fished upstream, dead drift, or downstream on a mended line. Besides connecting you with angling history, they connect you with trout! My favorites are the Partridge and Green, and the Partridge and Orange.

Running swiftly as they do, and offering fish both little time to look at their food as it whisks by and a pretty fair variety of insect life, San Juan streams allow the fisherman a good deal of latitude in selecting flies. This is often not the case in high altitude lakes and ponds. There are two problems which often must be solved by the high lake fisherman if he is to be successful. He must first find the trout, and then he must find out what they are eating. The subject can be complex, but a few general rules apply.

Golden Stonefly, Nymph

Steven J. Meyers Photograph

Wooly Worm, Nymph

Trout can often be found at inlets, places where streams flow into lakes, and at outlets, places where lakes flow into streams. My experience is that it is generally fruitless to search open water for trout with a fly, unless, of course, there is something about the bottom structure which you have discovered which leads you to suspect that it harbors feeding fish. Local information often helps in this case.

A favorite little lake of mine has a channel which winds from its inlet to its outlet, hidden, underwater. I found it accidentally while fishing streamers with the countdown method and a fast retrieve one evening when I got tired of catching seven and nine inch brookies who were noisily feeding on the surface near shore. The countdown method involves casting a sinking line (or a weighted fly on a long leader—this technique not working as well as a sinking line), and counting before beginning the retrieve. The count is lengthened with each cast until a strike is felt. Continuing to cast and count to the number where the strike was received before beginning the retrieve usually results in more strikes. Trout often hold at a specific depth. The depth is determined by many things, but the two most important factors are the temperature of the water and the presence of food. Finding one fish underwater usually means finding several. The count allows you to control the depth at which your fly will be fished, and allows you to show it to more trout.

My countdown exploration of this particular lake placed my fly in a deep channel which was previously unknown to me. After my first strike, I explored the extent of the channel at the same depth by counting to the same number. Subsequent casts and retrieves brought me four beautiful wild brook trout in the fourteen to sixteen inch range. All were larger, stronger and healthier than any I had previously caught in the lake. When I told a friend, an old timer who has fished well and long in the same lake, he said, "Oh yeah, haven't I ever told you about that channel?" My advice then, regarding lakes, is to probe the inlets and outlets, count down where you suspect fish holding structures, pray a lot, and ask around. Some folks are kind enough to share their secrets.

As for flies, many seem to work. When trout are seen feeding on the surface, small flies often work best. I suspect that there are more midges in the lakes around here than anything else. Often imitations of midge pupae fished in the surface film do well. Some I know fish mosquito imitations religiously. If possible, strain the water surface with a fine net or piece of cloth and see what you can find there, then fish the closest thing you have in your fly box.

Below the surface it can be more difficult, but a few flies seem to work better than others when you are in doubt. Dragon fly nymphs do well. Generally imitative nymphs which suggest a broad range of underwater life also do well. Sometimes it is a good idea to fish several sizes and colors (light, medium and dark) until you receive a strike. Once again, try to get some information from a local who has fished the lake. The kinds of insects (and non-insect forage like scuds and fairy shrimp) often vary widely from lake to lake.

Steven J. Meyers Photograph

Squirrel Tail, Streamer

15

Lake fishing with the fly presents a unique and sometimes difficult challenge. While trout often feed in the shallow water near shore, often they do not. Fortunately, many of the lakes in the San Juans are accessible by automobile, which means they are also accessible to the canoe. The canoe allows a fisherman to cover more water, to move quickly when fish are spotted feeding, to do so quietly, and to choose the position from which he would prefer to cast. These advantages are not always available to the wading fisherman. The rhythm of the paddle is not unlike that of the flyrod, and it is a rare angler who, having found pleasure in fishing the fly, would not also find it in paddling. More than one blank fishing day has been redeemed by the simple joy of being on a mountain lake with paddle and canoe.

Steven J. Meyers Photograph

Perhaps the most extreme examples of selectivity I have seen have been in beaver ponds. True selectivity is fairly rare anywhere. It is extraordinary rare in the San Juans, but in my favorite early season beaver pond, it is the rule and not the exception. Usually you can intimidate a holding trout into striking out of territorial aggressiveness by repeatedly pulling a streamer past its snout, but this is not a particularly pleasant way to fish. Once, having fished for hours without a strike, I resorted to the technique, casting into a deep portion of the pond which I knew to hold fish in order to find out what was going on. After a few missed strikes, I finally hooked a fairly large brook trout in the lip. He was sacrificed, and his stomach contents examined.

Inside I found a mass of insects, all identical. Gently washing the mass in water on my palm, I discovered hundreds of chironomid pupae. Midges, and nothing else. I switched to a midge pupae imitation, and still had difficulty catching fish, the number of naturals present was so overwhelming that an imitation had little chance of being noticed, but I did catch fish, and I am certain that I caught more than I would have if I had not discovered how selective the feeding actually was.

So much for flies. What about rods, reels and lines? For the most part I doubt that recommendations on these matters are very important. Flies can be very regional and specific, but rods, reels, lines and their selection seem to have more to do with the

17

Partridge and Orange, Soft-hackled Wet Fly

personality, temperament and quirks of the fisherman than anything out there on the trout stream. Want to know my quirks? Here they are.

I like long rods. Not too long mind you, but I see almost no legitimate use for a rod under eight feet, and while I own a nice graphite eight footer for four and five weight line, as well as a fine bamboo seven-and-a-half footer which was originally made to throw an HDH line, I almost never fish them any more. Such rods were intended, I am told, for fishing small streams and small flies. This I do quite often, but I find that an eight and a half foot graphite rod gives me much more line control, and rarely does the extra half foot cause me any trouble in the brush. Much San Juan fishing is small stream fishing, and some of it involves large rivers, like the Animas. Personallly, I like to fish almost everything with my eight and a half foot rod which casts a weight forward six line beautifully, and also handles a double tapered five as well. For the beginner all of this talk might sound a bit technical, but really it is quite simple.

All rods act as springs, bending to store energy, and recoiling to release it. All rods, in addition, are designed to cast a certain weight of line, this being the weight which best matches the physical properties of the rod. Too heavy a line will bend the rod too much, greatly slowing down its motion, and possibly damaging the rod in the process. Too light a line will fail to bend the rod enough, and insufficient energy will be stored in the rod. What is most important is that a line be matched to a rod. The difficulty of doing this, for beginners, has been eliminated by tackle manufacturers who now mark a number on all fly rods which indicates what line weight will best match the rod. Some rod materials and designs will effectively cast a wide range of line

weights, and these rods are marked accordingly. All fly lines now sold also have a number on them which indicates the weight of the line. Balancing a rod to a line, for a beginner, simply means matching the number on the rod to that on the line. Later, with experience, a beginner learns that the length and speed of the cast significantly alter the loading of the rod, and affect decisions regarding line weight and rod weight. When you have gotten to this point the manufacturer's recommendations become guidelines, not iron clad rules.

Line weights readily available run from two to twelve, with two being the lightest. Lines at the ends of this scale have extremely specialized and limited use. A two weight system might make fishing size 24 flies to sipping trout a real treat. A twelve weight rig would be nice if you were off the coast of Central America fishing for tackle busting tarpon. Trout lines generally fall in the four to seven weight range. I own lines in the four to nine weight range. I do ninety percent of my fishing with fives and sixes. I believe these weights will serve well for most San Juan fishing, except for deep water nymphing in the largest rivers during runoff which might best be fished with a seven weight rig, or extremely small fly fishing to surface feeding trout where a four weight rig might appear more suitable. Actually, with an adequately long and properly tapered leader, it should be possible to fish even the smallest flies with the relatively heavy six weight line and rod. I am beginning to wonder if we really need to have ten rods in order to feel that we are adequately equipped. The best anglers I know generally fish one or two rods, and fish them well in all conditions. Come to the San Juans with a five or six weight setup, and know how to use it, and I doubt there will be anything that you won't be able to handle.

Guinea and Hare's Ear, Soft-hackled Wet Fly

Having said that, I must confess that I have a nine-footer for seven weight line that I love for fishing the lakes from a canoe, and sometimes I go out with my antique split bamboo seven-and-a-half footer, knowing that it is probably not the most efficient tool for the job, but because I love its look and feel, its rhythm, so. Oh well, who ever said that a fisherman had to be consistent!

Reels are, perhaps, as personal as rods and the decisions about what to buy probably based more on temperament and aesthetics than anything else. Anglers like to brag about the fight they encounter in their home trout. I'm no exception, but in all honesty I must admit that only one San Juan trout ever took out all of my fly line, and actually ran into my backing (a kokaneee salmon once took all of my line out several times, and much backing also, but that was on the edge of the San Juans in Blue Mesa Lake, and the first lightning fast run had the speed of a drifting canoe added to that of the fish). I never did see the San Juan trout that cleared my reel of line. He broke me off. I spread some rumors about Nessie's cousin being in the lake, but no one believed me. The point of this is that fishing in the San Juans does not require a reel with drag that will stop a truck, or withstand repeated runs into the backing. I would suggest the lightest strongest reel you can find that has adequate capacity for your line and perhaps fifty yards of backing (rough hiking will probably do more damage to equipment than hundred yard runs from the fish). The backing is there in the rare event that a trout will run out all of your line, but more important, to give your line a larger arbor on which to rest. The backing enlarges the effective diameter of the reel spools's center, and increases the amount of line you can retrieve with each turn of the handle. In addition, it keeps the end of your expensive flyline from becoming kinked and ruined on the small arbor of the reel spool. Should you have money for only one reel, and anticipate steelheading in British Columbia, or bone-fishing in Costa Rica (what are you doing traveling around the world if you only have money for one reel?) get a big reel with capacity for three hundred yards of backing, salt-water resistant construction, bomb proof drag, and be prepared to feel your wrist ache as you try to lift it while fishing for trout on a small mountain stream. Frankly, I hate automatic reels, but I know a good number of old timers who swear by them. If it is light, strong, won't jam when line is going out, and has enough capacity without going overboard, it is probably just fine for the San Juans. A hundred dollar English reel is a wonderful piece of machinery, and a beautiful thing to hold. If I could afford it, I'd have twenty. I doubt they'd help me catch any more fish though.

Earlier I mentioned the potentially obsessive nature of flyfishing for trout. There are many ways for the obsession to manifest itself. One is the neurotic love of the equipment flyfisherman use. Some would rather have fifty rods, fifty reels, and fifty mahogany flyboxes than spend fifty days on the

Dark Cahill, Wet Fly

stream. These we affectionately call gearheads. Others have learned fifty sub-species of mayfly, their Latin names and the number of segments and tails which constitute their abdomens, but whose own abdomens show a bit too much flab from having spent more time looking at pictures of bugs in books, than swatting them while hiking to remote streams. These we affectionately call taxonomical anglers. Others collect angling literature until the books fill warehouses; still others tie obscure and difficult patterns of extinct, or nearly so, mayflies, questing after just the right hackle cape, the perfect patch of urine stained belly fur from a female fox. This last, I think, legitimately constitutes a clinical obsession.

Embarrassed, I must admit that a little of each of these disgusting illnesses resides within me. None, however is my true obsession. This obsession consists in the fear that all time spent somewhere other than on a trout stream is somehow wasted. Is my tongue firmly planted within my cheek? Perhaps. Sometimes I wonder. There is little that I do which is not at some point interrupted by the desire to be on a trout stream somewhere. Dr. Freud, no doubt, would find this an interesting case, but were he alive in Vienna today he would have a tough time getting me out of the San Juans long enough to examine me. Some illnesses are, well, rather pleasant, and this is not one for which I will soon be seeking a cure.

Like many in the San Juans, beautiful Lime Creek, near Silverton, holds a variety of trout. Wild streambred natives live here, as well as wild populations of introduced trout, both rainbow and brook. In addition, this stream receives occasional plantings of hatchery reared rainbows. Relatively easy to catch, the hatchery fish provide fun and plenty of action. Catching one of the larger wild fish requires a bit more care. Necessary to some degree in all fishing, stealth becomes mandatory if the hope is to catch a wild trout. Wild trout of fourteen inches, and sometimes more, can be caught here, but success depends upon careful stalking, accurate casting and the ability to read water. A local angler demonstrates these qualities as he searches the limpid water for elusive wild trout.

Steven J. Meyers Photographs

Locomotive Number 461 is a smaller class K-27 engine in comparison to the larger power used on the Durango & Silverton Narrow Gauge today. She is shown ready for departure from Durango with a ''Mixed'' freight and passenger, Silverton bound. A second locomotive, ''cut'' into the middle of the train, acted as ''Helper.'' The passenger section brought up the rear. This photo was made during the 1950s when the Rocky Mountain Railroad Club sponsored trips, which promoted the train to the public. This promotion subsequently brought overflow crowds, attempting to ride the train, to Durango.

The 45.2 mile section of 3-foot gauge rail that yearly carries close to 150,000 tourists from Durango to Silverton and back is the one remaining piece of Colorado trackage of a once vast narrow gauge empire. The empire of 3-foot tracks once honeycombed the state from the frontal range to the Utah and New Mexico borders, and most areas in between. There were over a dozen roads that had the 3-foot gauge tracks, and between them there were well over a thousand miles of track, thousands of locomotives, freight and passenger cars, yards, shops, water tanks, coal tipples, bridges, tunnels, stations and other assorted paraphernalia necessary for the carrying of millions of tons of freight, ore and passengers each year during the boom years. Tracks were threaded around pre-

Three Feet

cipitous ledges that overlooked chasms of incredible depths. The rails were built into the high parks where the minerals were making prospectors and prostitutes alike rich beyond their wildest dreams. The shiny rails crossed raging streams and flat, dry deserts, always with the goal of reaching the rich camps that had sprung up in some of the most unlikely places. The 3-foot gauge cars carried whiskey, coal, machinery, madams, foodstuffs, and supplies in, and returned with the wealth of the mines. Colorado became world famous for its tiny railroads and the enormous riches that were being extracted from its mines.

The story goes, although it is probably apocryphal, that the founder of the Rio Grande, General William Jackson Palmer, chose 3-foot gauge because it was so narrow that it would be impossible to build a double width sleeper. He thought that narrow-gauge would forestall any immorality between consenting, but unmarried members of the opposite sex who might want to copulate while riding a railroad train. The main reason was, I am sure, that the General simply realized that 3-foot gauge was a lot cheaper than standard (4' 8½'') gauge to build, and that the rolling stock and locomotives were also a lot cheaper. Each cross tie (there is usually one every 18'' to 2 feet) is 2 feet narrower, and in a system of substantial proprotions, that alone makes for a big savings. When one considers that, of necessity, the rolling stock and motive power also must be lighter due to smaller proportions, the rail need be less heavy also. Considering that the ''baby'' railroad originated in Denver and then proceeded south to Colorado Springs, and then Pueblo, it certainly encountered no severe grades or sharp curves. It ran along in front of the mountains, rather than through them. There was no real reason for the 3-foot gauge choice other than economy.....unless he really was afraid of almighty vengeance being cast upon him for making it possible for illicit sex to be performed in his cars.

However, as the rich carbonate ores were discovered in the high peaks to the west, and when it was realized that the railroad that would serve those mining camps would have to put up with not only tortuous grades, but equally tortuous curves, I am certain that the railroad was glad it was in the 3-foot gauge business. Not that a narrow-gauge train can climb a more severe grade than a standard-gauge train, because it can't. But it can certainly negotiate sharper curves, and when scaling a mountain pass, it is very important to be able to gain elevation by constantly curving around. Narrow gauge's ability to make sharp curves allowed it to climb, it seemed, almost to the sky, by twisting and turning and

reversing itself over and over again, until a certain pass was accomplished, and then proceed to do the same thing on the other side to go down. The names of Lizard Head, Monarch, Cumbres, Marshall, and Cerro Summit, not to mention Boreas, Trout Creek and Kenosha, often bring tears of fondness to students of narrow gauge lore in Colorado. In various other states, such as Ohio, Michigan and Pennsylvania, there were 3-foot gauge railroads, but none have ever fostered the adoration and genuine affection that the Colorado narrow gauge railroads have and continue to inspire.

The undisputed ''Narrow-Gauge Capital of the World,'' was Silverton, which served as the terminus for four separate railroads, the Silverton Railroad, Silverton Gladstone and Northerly, Silverton Northern, and the Rio Grande. Prosperity was so great, that at one time, it was possible to book a sleeping car on a 23 mile long railroad that ended in Silverton, and have it transferred to the Rio Grande, with a destination of Denver, 497 miles away by rail. Otto Mears' Silverton Railroad was charging $1.00 per passenger mile, and doing a lusty business! This was 75 years ago, when the dollar bill could rightly be said to be sound, not inflated to virtual worthlessness as it is today. At a dollar per passenger mile, by today's standards, it was comparable to paying over $20,000 to cross the country on AMTRAK!

The Silverton Railroad began at Silverton and gradually went up in altitude until it reached Red Mountain Town, just a hundred yards from where U.S. 550 today crosses Red Mountain Pass at 11,016 feet. The line then descended into a wealthy basin surrounded by Red Mountains #1, 2 and 3, where dozens of spectacular producers were located, such as the Yankee Girl, Commodore, and today's Idarado. Through a series of switchbacks and by means of a covered turntable, which was the darling of the engineering fraternity then, the line reached the now ghost town of Ironton. From Ironton, it went a couple of miles further to Albany, where a few houses still remain. The Silverton Railroad's grades and remains are easily visible, even to the untrained eye, along the ''Million Dollar Highway'' that runs from Ouray to Silverton (so called because it is said that the gravel used to build it contained a million dollars worth of precious metals). The Silverton ran until 1923, when the clock ran out and the rails came up.

A less prosperous, but much longer lived road that also originated in Silverton, was the Silverton Northern. It lasted until the 1940's and regularly served the mines north of Silverton, as well as the towns of Howardsville, Eureka, and even as far as the Forks of the Animas. Animas Forks, three miles

To Silverton

by Don Stott

This bird's eye view of Durango was photographed from a hill south of town showing the yards and terminus of the Durango & Silverton Narrow Gauge Railroad. One can follow the course of the Animas River through town and out at the upper right hand corner of the photograph. The railroad follows the course of this river to Silverton.

Ron Ruhoff Photograph

Steven J. Meyers Photographs

above Eureka, had such steep grades (7%), that a locomotive was able only to push three cars up and let down four, lest it's air brakes be insufficient and there be a terrible runaway. Photos exist showing tiny trains plowing through snow drifts twice as high as their engine stacks, and the ever present avalanche danger was constantly on everyone's mind. The remains of this line can still be seen by everyone. The enginehouse and station still exist in Silverton, as do the easily identified grades north of town.

Northwest of Silverton ran the Silverton, Gladstone and Northerly, which was acquired by Otto Mears shortly after its completion. It was run up the canyon carved out by Cement Creek, and today some of its trestles and bridges are still visible from the nicely maintained gravel road that runs along its route. This was the first of the three to disappear, not surviving even the year 1918. Much data, photos, schedules, dining car menus, and remains are available for the student of railroading to view. But, of course, without the Denver and Rio Grande's line from Durango to Silverton, none of the three little lines could possibly have ever existed, nor could the huge mining boom have occurred. Cheap rail

A clear fall morning in 1975 finds Denver & Rio Grande Western locomotive Number 478 pulling out of Durango station for a run to Silverton. Private Car "William Jackson Palmer" is seen in the background (the photo on pages 24-25 was taken from the top of the hill also seen in the background).

Ron Ruhoff Photograph

transport is vital to the efficient operation of an industrial or mining business. The line left Durango in 1881 and arrived in Silverton amidst much celebrating on July 9, 1882. It is said that the hangovers on July 10th were such that the entire town was virtually paralyzed. Shiny rails that are laid just 3 feet apart on 6 foot ties placed on bare earth, have hauled billions of tons of freight over the last 105 years, not to mention millions of people. Of course, the end is no where in sight now that the line from Durango to Silverton has been acquired and lovingly restored by one Charles Bradshaw, a Florida nabob and railroad lover par excellence. Now, each summer, four trains full of happy riders arrive in Silverton each day, their combined passenger count often exceeding 2,000. Along the way, these lucky riders stare in awe at the sheer drop of 1200 feet from the cliff of the "High Line," a view of which William Henry Jackson captured for posterity a hundred years ago with his ponderous view camera, after risking life and limb by descending into the canyon to expose a historic glass plate negative that still sells well each year.

The Silverton line has wondrous scenery to behold from the train, regardless of which side one sits on in either the closed or open cars. I always prefer the open myself, even though my state of cleanliness might be suspect at the end of the line in Silverton, due to the constant working of steam by the locomotives, necessitated by the fact that the entire trip from Durango to Silverton is uphill. The downhill return trip is far more conducive to a clean head and shirt than the upward Silverton climb. Along the line is the Garfield monument, which marks the spot at which a train was located when news of the President's assassination was received. A dude ranch, Ah Wilderness, and a five star resort, Tall Timbers, are also on the line, and are not accessible by any means other than railroad in summer. Above Tall Timbers, and near the Garfield Monument, is a rather flat area where Purgatory Creek flows into the Animas River. This is the site of the colossal train wreck which was staged during the filming of the movie "Denver and Rio Grande." Two old, virtually useless locomotives were steamed up for the last time and placed at opposite ends of the track. Nine cameras were turned on so as not to miss an angle. The crews opened their throttles wide and jumped. When the two engines came together, it was such an awesome and spectacular "cornfield meet," that the film is still worth watching just for that scene. There was such a great amount of flying debris from this thunderous explosion, that it was being picked up for years afterwards. So much junk was laying around, that the railroaders gave the area the name of "Scrap Metal Junction," and some still refer to it by that name.

A heavy wet snow blanketed Hermosa as this work train moved toward Rockwood with two cabooses in tow. Mr. Bradshaw demonstrates himself to be a good provider for his crews with the coal fired stoves and bunks seen in this view taken in 1981. The scenic Hermosa Creek bridge was built in 1936 as a wooden pony Howe truss structure with a span of 64 feet.

Dell A. McCoy Photographs

Busy with work train movements in the fall of 1985, Hermosa saw much action. Here we see former East Broad Top steel hopper cars being used to ballast the line toward Silverton. A front end loader was used to fill the cars with gravel dumped on the ground from trucks.

Before reaching Rockwood, the track passes Shalona Lake and by this scenic rock wall, seen here receiving the warming rays of the morning sun.

During the fall of 1985, this activity at Rockwood was photographed as a work train came off the "high line" with empties headed for Hermosa. The crew chose to wye the locomotive and caboose by uncoupling the locomotive, turning her on the wye, and then running backward to pick up the caboose. Then the

locomotive ran forward again, and shunted the caboose which slowly ran free to the tail of the wye. The locomotive then gathered the empty drop bottom cars, coupled onto the caboose and departed for Hermosa.

William P. Price Photograph

This work train was photographed on October 1, 1962 as it passed the cliffs a few hundred yards south of Rockwood. It was loaded with replacement rail to be used on the line farther north.

This fairly recent photograph of the ''high line'' was made in July, 1985. It shows Durango & Silverton Narrow Gauge train Number 463 as it inches its way along the precarious shelf, some four hundred feet above the roaring rapids of the Animas River. The climb down to the spot from which the photo was taken is extremely difficult, and permission to do so must be granted by the D&SNG.

Ron Ruhoff Photograph

The famous "high line" (just a short hike north of Rockwood) is a place where the railroad grade was literally cut out of the rock. Here a work train returns to Hermosa with empty former East Broad Top steel hopper cars. Recently the grade had a washout at this location which was repaired and reinforced with steel.

Dell A. McCoy Photographs

In this photograph one of the morning trains headed for Silverton slowly worked her way out onto the "high line" as passengers in the luxurious "Alamosa" parlor car enjoyed the view. The "Alamosa", complete with bar and table seating may be ridden for a separate ticketing charge. On the opposite page, D&SNG locomotive Number 497 (a former standard-gauge locomotive) is shown drifting off the "high line" into Rockwood in the late afternoon.

ABE (4)
20.00
2242
51.11
65.N

Dell A. McCoy Photograph

Many other movies have been filmed in the area. The most famous was probably Mike Todd's spectacular, "Around the World in 80 Days." Several segments of the narrow-gauge line were used, including Rockwood, the "High Bridge," and the area near Ignacio. The red, white and blue railroad station that appeared when the sail car was used, was the Ignacio Station. It kept its colorful garb until the line was abandoned in 1970 and a few years later was moved from the site. The collapsing bridge scene was filmed utilizing trick photography on the Rockwood High Bridge located between the Tacoma power plant and the famous High Line. The "tunnel" was formed by covering the high rocks on either side of the track just after leaving Rockwood, with a paper mache top. Locomotive #315 was used in the movie. It now sits at the Durango Chamber of Commerce on the bypass near route 160. Other movies include, "Ticket to Tomahawk," which featured a wooden dummy engine being pulled up Blair Street in Silverton, "Night Passage," and "Great Day in the Morning." In many of these movies, little kids can be seen as extras, or perhaps sitting on Jimmy Cagney's knee. These youngsters have now grown into adults and have many fond memories of their childhoods in Silverton, and on occasion, performing in real Hollywood movies.

A hydro power plant was built along the tracks just below Ah Wilderness guest ranch in 1906, which used the waters from a lake high above. It has faithfully produced electricity ever since, and it too, is only accessible by rail. There used to be a little station by the Tacoma Plant many years ago with a sign that said "Tacoma, population - 18, more or

41

A guard rail gives a feeling of security as trains traverse the "high line" above the Animas gorge.

less." Today the power plant maintains its own fleet of gas powered rail cars for access entering and egress between the plant and the outside world. Just below the Tacoma plant is the so called High Bridge, that spans the rushing Rio de Las Animas Perdidas (River of Lost Souls). The tracks stay relatively level while the river loses elevation very rapidly, and the combination results in the High Line, which some say is the most spectacular view from any train anywhere in the world. The train snakes around sharp curves high above the river on a narrow ledge carved from a cliff. The engineer sometimes appears to be directly across from you as you are at the rear of the train, separated only by a sheer drop to the bottom of the canyon. The trip from Durango to Silverton is well worth the time and money!

Ron Ruhoff Photograph

Conductor Alva Lyons once made his way through the train, punching tickets as the flanged wheels squeeled in protest against the tight curves near Rockwood. In the photograph below, a special train chartered in 1964 by the Rocky Mountain Railroad Club carries the prominent figure, Otto Perry, who is seated in the front row, second from the left.

Ron Ruhoff Photograph

The morning passenger train to Silverton, headed by locomotive Number 481, is shown here crossing a cast-iron, deck-truss bridge which is 130 feet long. The bridge which was originally built in 1894 was strengthened by Mr. Bradshaw in 1981 in order to allow the passage of heavier locomotives. On the next page the parlor car "Alamosa" can be seen bringing up the end of this train. Below, on the right, a "pop-car" owned by and lettered, "Colo Ute", is seen coming in off the "high line" in the late afternoon, behind the passenger trains.

Dell A. McCoy Photographs

For many years, the Denver and Rio Grande, as it progressed across the vastness of Colorado, had a rather nasty habit of blackmailing the various towns it proposed to serve. As the railroad approached Canyon City, Pueblo or Animas City, for example, delegates from the railroad would approach the various town fathers and demand money to help defray the costs of construction, and in return for this money, the railroad agreed to build into the town and virtually guarantee prosperity. Sometimes the towns paid and all was rosy. Other times, as in the case of Animas City, the town decided that it wanted no part of the pressure play, and declined the invitation to pay for service. As usual when such happened, the railroad went about planning its own town, usually a couple of miles away. In the case of Animas City, it was Durango. Animas City was prospering. It had a nice, brisk trade with the surrounding miners to the west in the La Platas, and from the farmers and dairymen who had settled the rich, fertile valleys nearby. Who could ask for more? Why pay that damned railroad to build. It will hurt the railroad, not Animas City! They will come begging to US! At least that was the way it was supposed to happen. So Animas City declined, and the railroad laid out a town and called it Durango, at the suggestion of a railroad official who had just returned from Mexico, and fancied the name. Durango it was to be.

The streets were laid out, and the railroad kept all of the property between the tracks and the Animas River. A suitable yard, roundhouse, and station were built and all waited for the first train, which duly arrived in early 1881. Lot sales were brisk, and soon the population of Animas City was moving down to Durango. Durango prospered and Animas City ceased to exist. About the last anyone ever heard of Animas City, was when the Durango streetcar system listed Animas City as one of its destinations. The trolleys went out in 1921. Today, Animas City would be located at about 32nd Street and Main Avenue, in the modern, colorful town of Durango. Durango was also the southern terminus of a little railroad that ceased to exist in the early 1950's after close to 75 years of starving, patching, begging and hoping. The Rio Grande Southern was the brain-child of Otto Mears. It ran for close to 175 miles in a wildly circuitous route that eventually ended at Ridgway, nine miles north of Ouray. The line went through vast unpopulated areas, over tortuous Lizard Head Pass, and traversed the spectacular, spindly bridges at Ophir. From there, the line went down and into Telluride, which was named for the rich tellurium ores found in adjacent mines. From Telluride, the rails clung to mountains, passed Placerville, went up over Dallas Divide and down into Ridgway. The Rio Grande Southern limped along through the years with loans, luck, bailing wire, and a sheer determination to survive, that might be characteristic of a man afloat on a raft in the middle of the ocean. Finally, it was ended, after the brief glorious moment when the Rio Grande Southern hauled out of the shining mountains the

uranium used to make the bombs that were dropped on Japan to end World War II. Remains of this colorful line are everywhere to be seen as you drive over this route. The Rio Grande Southern entered Durango from the west, very close to what is now U.S. Highway 160.

The Rio Grande also built south from Durango into New Mexico. The line ended at Farmington. Traffic looked so promising that the Farmington branch was standard-gauged in 1905. Most thought this was a prelude to total standard gauging of the line from Alamosa to Silverton. But it was not to be, and the line was returned to narrow gauge in 1922. For a few years, the yards of Durango sported both standard gauge as well as narrow gauge tracks. By 1970, all tracks had been abandoned out of Durango, except the line to Silverton, which as early as 1950 had caught the eye and patronage of the rail fan and tourist who realized that the line offered some of the most spectacular scenery anywhere in the world. Gone are the lines to Farmington and Telluride. Gone is the line from Durango to Chama, which was the link to the outside world for the entire Southwestern Colorado area ... by rail.

Over the many years, the snows have snarled the Silverton line, just about as regularly as Dad has his morning coffee. When Charlie Bradshaw bought the Durango-Silverton line in 1980, he decided that the line would be kept open the year round, and proudly announced to a group of Silvertonians that they shouldn't be at all surprised if they saw trains running year round, winter and summer. The first winter gave the crews fits and it just wasn't economically feasible. Light engines were sent to buck the drifts at the common disaster points, namely at Mileposts 492 and 492.5. These mark the spots of the infamous Snowshed and Cleveland slides, which of course, are avalanche paths. The valiant 478 came back to Durango late one evening with a snowplow that was horribly bent out of shape, and we all knew that the fight had been lost by the players in the 1980's. It was really of no concern, as the life support items such as food, fuel, mail and supplies no longer traveled by rail, but highway, and the railroad had become but a wonderful tourist attraction.

Not too many years before this last effort to keep the line open, it was a yearly life and death struggle. Especially before 1950. The stories of heroic efforts by hundreds of able bodied men to hand shovel the immense drifts off the tracks, while shivering Silvertonians waited, is the material of thriller movies and novels. The Snowshed slide got it's name because a heavy timber snowshed was erected by the railroad

The impressive deck-truss bridge was missing guard rails between the tracks as the road was being upgraded with new rail and ballast when this 1982 photograph was made.

in the early part of the century, and it worked well. That left the Cleveland. The Snowshed was a massive structure, built with huge squarecut timbers that were so placed as to be self supporting and would defy the mightiest slide. When the D&RGW destroyed it in 1949, it was said to be still in good condition, but it's destruction removed it from the tax rolls, and would also aid in the continual effort to abandon the line, efforts which began, believe it or not, in 1919.

When the Silverton line went down due to the slides in the canyon, it left Silverton babies without milk in later years, but it left Silverton's milk cows without hay and straw in earlier years. Silverton, you see, had several dairies which operated year round. Obviously, hay doesn't grow in Silverton at any time of the year, but certainly not in winters when Baker's Park is snowed in with a vengeance. The dairy men used to ship their hay in by rail to keep their cows alive and producing. When the eternal snows stopped up the narrow canyon and prohibited rail movement, there were many "bossies" in Silverton who would have starved, if the trains couldn't get moving pretty quickly. One especially hard winter found the canyon blocked so tightly, that it took over 40 days to break it free. By then, if it hadn't been for the ingenuity of Silverton's dairymen, and the dedication of the United States Postal Service, they would have all starved. What the Silvertonians did, was to MAIL the hay from Durango! Even though the costs were astronomical, it was pay or die, so sufficient hay was sent to the post office and postage affixed. It took post office employees on snowshoes to haul that hay into Silverton. It cost the U.S. government a bundle, and was a tribute to the ingenuity of Silvertonians. Before the canyon got open, food was getting low, as was coal, and when the first whistle was heard, a great shout of relief was heard around the town. It was also timely, because supplies of whiskey were dropping alarmingly as well!

There were two ways of getting the canyon open: shoveling it clear, or tunneling through. In severe slides, shovelers merely shoveled a tunnel through the massive pile, which many times would be close to 100 feet deep. The problem with tunneling, was that as warm weather came, the tunnel would collapse onto the tracks, burying them again. But the trains had to go through, and it took a lot of manpower to keep the vital line open. Until almost the end, when the Silverton Northern track was taken up, the shovelers were hauled to the slides by a Silverton Northern engine carrying them down the 6 miles of canyon to the work site. This saved the energies of the shovelers, At least they didn't have to walk to work. The slide was attacked on both sides, and at the end of the day, the Silverton Northern engine and cars would chug into town full of weary laborers, who collapsed from sheer exhaustion. They went back down the canyon next day. Imagine repeating this process each year several times, and sometimes for five weeks at a crack. All this to get the line open

Dell A. McCoy Photographs

The second morning passenger train, pulled by locomotive Number 476, eases out onto the deck-truss bridge spanning the Animas River in this 1982 view. In the photo above, the "Cinco Animas" brings up the rear of the train giving its riders an experience, and an adventure, 1880s style!

49

The station at Tacoma (elevation 7,313') provides access for the Colorado Ute Electric Association's Tacoma power plant. Electra Lake, 1,071 feet higher, provides the water for this plant built in 1905.

so that life giving supplies could be brought in and profits hauled out of the remote town. Winters have never been said to be easy in the high passes, and Silverton at 9318 feet, is one of the highest towns in the world. Leadville is a few hundred feet higher than Silverton, but has far less snow, due to it's geographical location. Leadville is also not surrounded by high peaks, as is Silverton, so it has winds that blow away a lot of snow. Silverton's surrounding mountains squeeze the clouds like a giant sponge, and the snow drops like lead pellets onto the miniscule town and surrounding canyons, which accumulate it and send it crashing down below in huge avalanches onto the Silverton line.

In some winters, old man snow doesn't get too mean and ornery. Other winters, such as the winter of 1905-06, were so severe that not only were the trains blocked for months, but extensive damage to mining properties was done by blizzards, the likes of which even the old timers hadn't seen. Many tram towers were knocked down by avalanches, the tracks were impassable, and an epidemic of pneumonia struck as well. With miners' lungs already full of rock dust, they were too weakened to withstand the ravages of pneumonia, and in the winter of 1905-06, there was an average of three deaths per week.

In 1980, when Charlie Bradshaw found that it was cost prohibitive to keep the line open to Silverton in the winter, he decided on another tack. He built a wye in the tracks right about the area of the famous

"Scrap Metal Junction," only he called it "Cascade." He began running winter trains from Durango up to Cascade and back until the winter of 1985. A quick look at the books, as well as passenger counts, indicated far too many trains with two, four, and sometimes no passengers on them, creating huge amounts of red ink. When the crew members outnumber the passengers, it isn't profitable. So the Cascade run in winters went to bed.

It might have been a little more feasible to keep the line open in winters if a rotary plow could have been used. A rotary snow plow is a steam powered blade on the front of a specially built car. The blade bites into the snow and throws it high into the air and clear of the blockage. Rotary plows are still used on parts of western railroads. I think of Donner Pass as an example where the Donner party froze to death a hundred plus years ago, not while riding a train, but while attempting to cross the high Sierras in the middle of winter, which was in itself most foolish. The problem with the rotary plow, is that it sort of self destructs when it comes into contact with anything much harder than snow. The slides at the snowshed were always full of trees, rocks, boulders, and all sorts of debris that avalanches are wont to carry with them when they break loose and thunder down a mountainside. So the rotary was out, even though it was tried occasionally.

Of course, any businessman has his or her detractors, and railroads are certainly not exempt.

Here the track crosses the Animas River on a cast iron bridge which was placed here in 1911. The track then passes Tefft, a sawmill site where ties and mine timbers were produced for the Cascade Creek area. Below, looking in a northeasterly direction, we catch a quick glimpse of the Needles Mountains (from left to right: Pigeon Peak, Turret Peak and Mount Eolus) before the train moves on.

Dell A. McCoy Photographs

51

The Needleton Tank was a mandatory stop on the long uphill run to Silverton. The Rocky Mountain Railroad Club chartered this excursion of Memorial Day 1966. A fine view of Mountain View Crest forms the backdrop. Today, water is stored and dispensed from a steel tank near the location of the original wooden tank.

Ron Ruhoff Photograph

No.36

60 FEET DEEP.
SAGUACHE SNOWSLIDE, ANIMAS CANON, NEAR SILVERTON
BRUMFIELD   PHOTO. OURAY.   COLO.

The current ownership of the line by Charlie Bradshaw has had a remarkable record of having virtually no detractors. But the Denver and Rio Grande Western was roundly despised and criticized by one and all. The first attempt at abandonment of the line was in 1919, and it never stopped until the sale to Bradshaw was completed for $2.2 million. The Rio Grande never really liked narrow gauge operations, and after World War II, it didn't like steam operations either. It was sad to see totally rebuilt locomotives hauled to the scrap yard in the fifties by the Rio Grande. The tax incentives were much higher if a new steam engine was scrapped than if an old one was scrapped. It wasn't the fact that the locomotive was worn out that led to scrapping. Many times it was virtually new. Off to the scrappers it went anyway. The Rio Grande wasn't the only railroad that participated in this carnage.

San Juan County Historical Society - Henry M. Doud Collection - Brumfield Photograph

Battles with snow on the line are legendary. This photograph of avalanche debris and the path which has been cleared through it gives a good idea of the dimensions of the struggle. The writing on the photograph proclaims this to be the Saguache snowslide, and the depth of the debris to be sixty feet!

The "Snowshed Slide" structure, which was 339 feet long, was built in 1890 to protect the track from avalanches which occur with fair regularity at this spot.

Lad G. Arend Photograph, Elmore Frederick Collection

In this photograph, taken early in the spring of 1983, locomotive Number 481
is seen heading for Silverton after clearing the famous "Snowshed Slide".

It is still spring of 1983 in this photograph, and locomotive Number 473 still has her snowplow attached. Debris from another slide holds on beside the Animas River, even though the weather has warmed.

Not far above the ''Snowshed Slide'' the track runs nearly straight for a short distance allowing an excellent view of Garfield Peak to the south.

This area north of Needleton is known as "Hunt's Spur". The track on the right is the original line, that on the left a shoo-fly used to circumvent the slide debris.

The Rio Grande did not want to bother with this incredible layout of steam powered narrow-gauge lines that for the most part easily paid its own way, and sometimes showed a profit. The lines were tucked away in remote parts of Colorado, serving little towns, and were the subject of books, photos, movies, and total adoration by thousands of the faithful who yearly went to the Centennial State to view the remains and ride last runs. The Rio Grande was merely interested in divesting itself of all that remained of the colorful and romantic history of Colorado narrow-gauge railroading. They were clever when they abandoned. They never did it whole hog. They would, for instance, abandon a key link of a narrow-gauge line. Say the link from Cimmaron to Montrose, or from Salida to Hooper, maybe. After a line was severed, it was easy to make it seem impossible to continue. Especially when the railroad had a common carrier truck line that always managed to be there to haul the freight at a much lower price than those bothersome little narrow-gauge railroads. The mail contract alone, made the run from Alamosa to Durango on the revered "San Juan" train, break even, and the passengers made it show a profit. But when the railroad went before the state P.U.C. to file for abandonment, it conveniently failed to mention the mail contract, and instead showed the horribly low passenger counts. When the San Juan went, it was easy to allow the line to fall into gradual disrepair. It was also easy to sidetrack desperately needed oil pipeline and drilling equipment for weeks, to make the railroad a hated transportation device by those who really needed it during the Farmington oil boom. Eventually, of course, the entire track between Alamosa and Durango and Farmington was abandoned in 1970.

The section between Chama and Antonito was quickly bought by the states of New Mexico and Colorado and has been preserved. It is being operated today as a tourist line. The sighs of relief in the Denver boardrooms were not hard to imagine when 200 miles of line went to dust and the scrapper. All that was left was that infernal Silverton line which those damned tourists insisted on riding. Each year the torrent of riders increased, and finally, through a court action, the Rio Grande was forced to operate a second train each day from Durango to Silverton. This left the sold out sign on display for perhaps only 75% of the time rather than 95%. Sold out periods then declined from most of the summer, to only 3 weeks in advance. Locomotives were held together with bailing wire and inept welds, it seemed, and I once paced the 478 from "Red Barn" to Hermosa in my diesel car. The diesel was noisy enough, but I honestly thought the poor 478 would disintegrate. It was clanking and rattling and hissing so badly, that if it weren't steam, it would have ceased to function years before. That 45.2 mile section of the once vast network of narrow-gauge lines just couldn't be made to show a loss, even though the Rio Grande charged off a portion of top Denver management to it's books.

In this downriver view, the morning train is but a few miles below Silverton. Garfield Peak on the western end of the Grenadier Range is visible in the left center, while some of the eastern peaks of the Needles Mountains are visible to Garfield's right.

In early September, 1970, it looked for a while as though they had it made. A severe rain kept on for days and days. Rivers rose to unprecedented heights and it still rained bucketsfull. Finally it got so bad and so high that a sudden cloudburst was all it took, and several miles of track, bank and grade were washed out. Service was suspended for the rest of the year. A quick application for abandonment was submitted to the P.U.C. in Denver. By this time, Durango was heavily dependent on the train for it's economic sustenance, and Silverton too had tasted the sweet fruits of the tourist dollar in it's cash registers. The P.U.C. said no, and the Rio Grande sullenly rebuilt, only to have to haul even more passengers in the summer of 1971. By 1980, it had grown absurd. The Rio Grande had a total of 16 cars and 3 engines that were in the worst of condition. As this is being written, in July of 1986, Bradshaw has changed all of this! There are six operable engines in superb condition, and a few others awaiting the loving hand of the roundhouse crew. There are 42 cars on the premises, most of them full each day on the four trains that enter Silverton. A new car shop has been erected in Durango and the finest, most skilled wood workers have been hired to fashion out of fine oaks and cherries, cars that outdo even those works of art that were produced by Jackson and Sharpe 100 years ago, and which still run on the line to Silverton. Each new car is exactly the same style, dimensions and appearance as an original and it takes a trained eye to differentiate. New steel frames are built by Telluride Iron Works in Durango, and even new trucks (the frames that wheels fit into) are being cast. Seat stanchions are being recast from originals that have been carefully remolded into forms for duplication. Tern roofs are carefully applied, as was the custom 100 years ago, and which is now virtually a lost art—not to mention expensive. Locomotives have had their number boards duplicated as original, and the phony balloon stacks were long ago removed. Everything is as it was when it was new, and new equipment is as it would have been when built in those days of yore, when the world turned a little more slowly, it seemed.

An excellent view of the Needles in snow (Turret Peak on the left, Pigeon Peak on the right) was recorded from this particularly scenic location a few miles below Silverton in the upper reaches of the Animas Canyon (compare this photograph with that on page 56).

In a photograph taken from the same location as that on the two previous pages, but looking to the north this time, Grand Turk Mountain rises above the Animas Canyon. The King Mine (opposite) cabled ore across the Animas River for loading onto cars at a spur.

Dell A. McCoy Photographs

These two photographs show Cataract Gulch during the spring runoff.

Dell A. McCoy Photographs

The narrowest portion of the Animas River canyon, just below Silverton, sometimes presents extraordinary photographic material, making it a railfan's paradise. All too often, the smoke from these hard working locomotives completely obscures the photographer's view. Below, the photographer had positioned himself near the edge of Cataract Falls. In this rather dangerous position he looked down on top of the D&RGW train as she squealed her flanges around this sharp curve.

Dell A. McCoy Photographs

While living in Silverton, the photographer was able to obtain many photographs of the trains in fresh snow. Number 481 is seen here plowing powder snow through the narrowest part of the canyon, just below Silverton, in 1982. This is very near the location to which track had reached by June 27, 1882. When the train whistle blows here, it can be heard in Silverton. These photographs record the passage of the train.

Dell A. McCoy Photographs

Decorated with the United States flag, and the Colorado state flag, 481 is seen here hauling the Governor Lamm special into Silverton in 1982. This train was run in recognition of the one-hundredth anniversary of track reaching Silverton. In the photograph on the opposite page, taken in the same location, we see the Animas River with her beautiful green summer color.

Dell A. McCoy Photographs

With less coal smoke obscuring the view, Cataract Falls becomes visible in this fall photograph. In the opposite photograph, a dusting of autumn snow greets train riders who have come on a double-headed train to see the fall colors. Two engines were used to pull the lengthy train on a day when one train was scheduled, but too many would be riders had unexpectedly bought tickets to be handled by a single locomotive.

One of the last trains of the season is seen leaving Silverton in the opposite view taken near the end of November in 1982. In the view above, clouds seem to hold Silverton captive on a cold, damp summer day.

Dell A. McCoy Photographs

An early, windy autumn in Silverton may strip the leaves from the aspen prematurely. Although it looks a bit like winter, the temperatures may still be balmy. A sure sign of winter's coming, however, is the gradual shortening of the trains.

76

Another trainload of fall color enthusiasts **had just pulled into Silverton** behind two locomotives when this image was made. **From here** the train's riders will spread throughout the town seeking **refreshment** in the eating establishments of Silverton, and spending time in the **many shops** and historic sites located there.

Dell A. McCoy Photographs

In November of 1982 this train rolled past the hundred year old Silverton depot, which, after a long hiatus, was once again being used by the railroad to sell tickets. C.W. McCall, a popular country and western singer who has recorded many songs about the San Juans, is seen in the photograph on the right arriving aboard the private car "Nomad" during United States bicentennial (and the Colorado centennial) celebrations in 1976.

The San Juan Express, an early morning train that runs during the peak of the summer season, is shown here returning to the end of track after turning on the wye. Earlier, she had arrived in town and discharged her passengers. Once turned around she will be ready for boarding passengers for the return trip to Durango. On the overleaf, the San Juan Express clatters by the Silverton depot during Sundance Publications' final year in the building. Some of the Sundance staff and a few visitors are seen enjoying the arrival of the train along with ticket agent, Allen Nossaman (on the left).

79

Winter nights and mornings can be extremely cold in Silverton, especially at the depot which is located near the river at one of the lowest points in town. This three minute time exposure shows the giant pot-bellied stove which is still used to provide much of the heat for the depot. It also shows a coach which was purchased by a Silverton resident for restoration. In the photo, below left, we see the depot, boarded up and without electricity, sewer or water, empty, before Sundance's occupation of the building in 1975. In the photo below the depot is pictured, occupied, held in the grip of winter in 1979.

Dell A. McCoy Photographs

These four views illustrate the feeling of winter at the depot, as snows accumulate, and thoughts and hopes of spring and the arrival of the first train begin to grow.

Dell A. McCoy Photographs

On these pages we see photographs of two different final days of the season in Silverton. In 1982, enough snow had fallen the previous night to be thrown by the wedge plow mounted on locomotive Number 481. In 1981 (lower right) a snowstorm had moved in dropping large wet flakes, and creating a dark and somber mood.

Dell A. McCoy Photographs

Since buying the Silverton line, Bradshaw has replaced many thousands of ties, built passing sidings, added thousands of tons of ballast (the uniform rocks that can be seen under the tracks that keep the track well drained and supported), and replaced old light rail with newer and heavier rail. The trains that used to threaten to derail between Durango and Hermosa on the long straight stretch of track due to crooked, unstable rail, now are smooth at more than twice the old speed limit imposed by the Rio Grande of 14 mph. Ticket sales have been computerized, and ticket sellers now know you are doing them a favor, rather than the reverse attitude of former days. The railroad advertises, and cares for it's riding customers now, rather than tolerating them as a necessary evil, because the P.U.C. in Denver refused to allow abandonment.

To be fair, it is rumored that even though the Rio Grande did apply for abandonment over and over again, the stockholders were said to be divided over the Silverton line. After 97% of the narrow-gauge had been successfully ripped up, with governmental permission, it is said that some on the board did want to do a good job in Durango, and make the line reflect the good name of the D&RGW as it operated in the rest of the state. The main line through the Rockies, which is still the Denver and Rio Grande Western, is a finely tuned piece of machinery, that has no peer as far as modern technology and efficiency is concerned. The line of the D&RGW that runs from Salt Lake City, east through the Rockies, is a wonder of man's achievement in the eternal fight against the elements. A few years ago, a tremendous mud slide near the little town of Thistle, in eastern Utah, blocked the line totally with an earthen dam, backed up by a steadily growing lake. Unable to break the dam, and realizing that the tracks beneath the water probably would never be seen again, the D&RGW went to work on a round the clock basis with the heaviest earth moving equipment and hang the expense. In a little over two weeks, and at huge cost, the line was reopened. It was a staggering accomplishment and a tribute to determination and modern earth moving technology. The Rio Grande always spent it's money on the main line, and virtually nothing on the narrow-gauges. Perhaps this strategy was partially understandable, but most businessmen would maintain anything that showed a profit. Perhaps a railroad is not an ordinary type of business.

With the arrival of a movie crew in Silverton in the fall of 1981, the railroad was pressed into service with an extra made up of freshly painted cattle cars. Many Silverton locals were used as movie extras in the shooting. The Silvertonians added local color to the film, but where the heck is Pine Meadows? (Editor's note: After several titles, including "The Return", and "Two Against the Wind" and trial releases, the movie never achieved great popularity. It has been seen recently circulating under the title "The Avengers."

Dell A. McCoy Photographs

The movie extra had a tough time attempting to move work train cars out of the Shenandoah siding. The cars' journal boxes were frozen from lack of use. Above we see movie actress Sherry Hursey, photographed from inside the depot, as she acted during filming. In the photograph below left, we see Ephram Zimbalist Jr., and other actors in the movie, aboard a carriage. Directly below, is a photograph of the movie extra in the morning sun.

Dell A. McCoy Photographs

Dell A. McCoy Photograph

Kendall Mountain dwarfs this freight train as it moves out of Silverton, and
down toward the canyon in 1982. Loads such as this were often destined for use
by mining and exploration projects within the canyon.

A freight load waited on the Shenandoah siding, early in the morning as the San Juan Express turned on the wye, as recorded in this 1983 photograph. In another photograph, made in 1982, Fritz Klinke, Silverton businessman and a promoter of the use of the railroad to haul freight, unloads plywood and other building materials from a boxcar at the Silverton depot.

A work train consisting of eleven drop bottom gondolas is loaded with ballast for tie replacement below Silverton in this 1985 photograph. During the fall season, when traffic on the line is reduced, Mr. Bradshaw had crews busy at both ends of the line bringing the grade up to first class condition.

Dell A. McCoy Photograph

The D&RGW had unloaded a mountain of ballast in the Silverton yard in preparation for repairs to the line. These two photographs show work trains being switched there in 1981 (left and below) and 1982 (right). A front-end loader was commissioned locally to fill the drop-bottom gondolas.

Dell A. McCoy Photographs

As a hopeless romantic, especially about railroads, and more especially about Colorado's narrow gauges, I used to weep bitter tears when I saw another link destroyed. My son, who is now an adult, learned to walk in the swaying cars on an Alamosa Kiwanis Club "Color Caravan," which ran each fall for many years. The train left Alamosa on a Friday morning, and some 12 hours later arrived in Durango. Saturday morning, the train left for Silverton, returning that same night. Sunday morning, it was back to Alamosa, arriving there Sunday night. I rode the "caravan" for five years, and then it was all over

for the vital link between Silverton and the main standard-gauge line. The Durango and Silverton line was isolated, with no physical connection of any kind by rail with the outside world.

The Rocky Mountain Railroad Club has, for more than 50 years, chronicled the comings and goings of the Colorado narrow-gauges. I have been a member for close to 30 years, as after riding into Silverton on a train in 1952 at age 18, I thought it wise to join. The Rocky Mountain Railroad Club, as well as the National Railway Historical Society, have always felt a special fondness for Southwestern Colorado's little

In November of 1981, passengers on the last train of the season had their lunch break cut short by an hour in order to insure that the track would not be blown shut down the canyon from Silverton. The train is seen here at the end of track after arriving in Silverton. Number 481, a class K-36 locomotive (the largest narrow-gauge locomotive built for the D&RGW) sits alongside Number 497, which was rebuilt from a standard-gauge C-41 and reclassed K-37, in the striking photograph below.

Dell A. McCoy Photographs

Still adorned in 1979 with the inaccurate diamond stacks placed on the loco-motives by the D&RGW, and despised by railfans and historians, locomotives filled the end of track to overflowing with railroad flavor—steam, coal smoke, leaking water, the clang of bells and the blowing of steam whistles.

3-foot lines. Hardly an occurrence has failed to be duly noted in various monthly newsletters or bulle-tins. In 1958, the late Lucius Beebe authored a volume of exquisite prose and rare photographs, and titled it "Narrow Gauge in the Rockies". The book has been a fabulous success, and many a rail affec-tionado has read it as a sort of "primer" on the subject of Colorado's Narrow-Gauges, and of course, especially the Silverton line, where the mountains meet the sky.

Tourists often ask how the locomotive will be turned around for the trip downgrade to Durango. A popular Silverton answer is that ten strong men will lift the locomotive, turn her around, and set her back on the track. Actually, the wye at the south end of town is used for this purpose, redirecting the entire train as a unit. In these photographs, we see several views of this turning process. Many times, the helper was cut out of the train during switching because the wye was not long enough to hold a long train and two locomotives. It would be turned separately, as seen in the photo above. In the upper right we see a work train drifting past, and below right, the morning San Juan Express backing to the wye.

Relative isolation characterized the hardships of the founding and early development of Silverton, just as it characterizes the experience of visiting the noted mining town today. And despite the remote nature of the 9,320-foot elevation historic community, time there can be as rewarding today as it was for many who began mining and brought the trappings of civilization to the town high in Southwest Colorado's San Juan Mountains.

Silverton, occupying a high mountain valley known as Baker's Park, is the surviving community from among many high altitude mining camps which existed in what is now San Juan County. It wasn't the first of the camps, but its relatively low altitude, plentiful water supply and room to grow made it the winner in the battle for supremacy among the settlements which dotted the creeks and hillsides in the rugged center of the San Juan Mountains.

Mining gave Silverton its start and sustained it

Silverton: "The Mining

The town of Silverton is seen across the Animas River looking toward Anvil Mountain from Kendall Mountain in this photograph taken in 1975. Two D&RGW trains are in town at mid-day, and a crush of sight-seeing tourists fills Silverton. At the time of this photo, the town of Silverton had few mobile homes or trailers. Several of the structures which appear in the photograph have disappeared (having burned, or been deliberately removed) or have been remodeled making the scene quite different from what it is today. The depot was, at that time, boarded up and unoccupied.

Dell A. McCoy Photograph

through the economic highs and lows of the last 112 years; and, although tourism has played an increasing role in the community's economic picture since the 1950s, Silverton is still a year-round mining town. The transition has been made from the initial prospectors—who came into the country with pick and burro and no capital—to large companies, absentee-owned, who are mining some of the same century-old mining claims with modern methods.

In between came almost unbelievably lean times,

including a dip in fortunes with the repeal of the Sherman Silver Purchase Act in 1893 and a period in the mid-1950s when those who were around talk about the only men doing manual labor being the three men who maintained the county roads.

The isolation was partially overcome in the early days when Silverton was targeted as the terminus of the longest single extension built by the Denver & Rio Grande Railroad. The entry of the narrow gauge railroad—built over a complicated route that even

Town That Wouldn't Quit"

by Allen Nossaman 103

Coming to Silverton from Durango on U.S. Highway 550, a magnificent panorama of Silverton emerges just before the road works its way down into the valley, and into town. Here we see Silverton bathed in late afternoon light. By this time most of the day-tripping tourists have left town; the mood and the tempo cool along with the temperatures. Boulder Mountain stands behind town at the intersection of Cement Creek and the Animas River. In the photograph above, we are looking back toward where the previous photo was taken. Grand Turk Mountain (on the left) and Sultan Mountain provide the background. The prominent towers in the photo belong to the Silverton Town Hall, and the San Juan County Building.

Dell A. McCoy Photographs

left the State of Colorado before it finally reached Silverton—transformed Silverton from a remote, struggling camp surrounded by mining prospects to a settlement that finally had a link to the outside world, which in turn meant a more feasible market for ores and easier access for the travelers and professional people who round out a town's existence.

The rails which connected the Silverton-to-

Durango segment of the narrow gauge with the rest of the Denver & Rio Grande system have been torn up, but this colorful branch line survives as an authentic relic of the past, carrying tens of thousands of tourists between Silverton and Durango each summer.

The first serious mineral prospecting in the Silverton area took place in 1860-61, by a variety of parties resulting from the promotional efforts of

Charles Baker, the namesake of Baker's Park. Most of the men involved were either California 49ers who had noticed and perhaps dabbled at prospecting in the mountains on their trek to the coast, or men disillusioned with the 1859 and 1860 results of work on Colorado's California Gulch—the eventual site of Leadville.

These parties were seeking placer gold, confining their search strictly to the creeks and streams of the high country. They found some placer evidence of the gold resources buried in vein form in the mountains—upon which others would later capitalize —and even built a few primitive sluices.

But, in addition to the fact that they were technically trespassing on Indian lands at the time, the advent of the Civil War back in the states brought an abrupt halt to the prospecting activity. There was a mass exodus from the San Juans, many suffering great hardships in winter crossings of the Continental Divide and many never realizing enough financially to have made the trek anywhere near worthwhile for them. Parties who brought trade goods in wagons and who might have been credited with great foresight in any other situation were forced to trade the goods to the Indians to bargain for safe passage out of the area.

The San Juans were basically devoid of Anglos for another ten years while the United States of America settled their differences and healed their wounds. Many who survived the Civil War, however, recalled their earlier adventures in the West, and among those were several who had been to Baker's Park on the Animas River and were anxious to return.

They did so in diverse parties starting in 1871. The Indian land trespass question became intensified by steadily increasing numbers of white men entering the San Juans in 1872 and 1873, and one in a long line of Indian treaties—the Brunot Agreement of 1873—removed the Ute Indians from the San Juan Mountain area around what was to become the site of Silverton.

The mountainous area could be, and had been, approached from any of a number of directions, but the prevalent route of access came to be the Stony Pass or Cunningham Pass route from the southeast. A supply center had grown up at Del Norte on the Rio Grande River during the first three years of the 1870s, and the inviting course of the Rio Grande presented relatively easy going to the new mining area deep in the San Juan Mountains, until one began to approach the Continental Divide. The going was rough, both going up and coming down once the range was reached; pack animals were often the only sure way to make the crossing for goods and men, and any wagons used were frequently either let down over certain portions by rope or disassembled in whole or in part.

Stony Pass and Cunningham Pass were two alternatives for crossing the divide on this Rio Grande route, and both ultimately led the traveler into Cunningham Gulch. Where this drainage intersected the Animas River, a highly informal settlement named Howardsville became the first county seat and the first post office west of the Continental Divide in Colorado in 1874. But Howardsville had limited space to grow and sprang up without benefit of platting or incorporation.

Where a few isolated cabins had been constructed in a much larger mountain park a few miles down the Animas River, another set of prospectors engaged an attorney and a surveyor and platted a town which was to become Silverton. By the fall election of 1874, Silverton had won the county seat designation away from Howardsville and was on its way to becoming the primary settlement of the area.

Other mining camps—some pre-dating the Silverton platting in 1874—dotted the hills. Many, such as Gladstone, Chattanooga and Needleton, enjoyed years of prosperity. Animas Forks boasted the only newspaper ever published outside of Silverton in the county. Eureka was transformed from an early thriving settlement into a company town that lasted well into this century. Others, like Poughkeepsie, Del Mino, Mineral Point and Niegoldstown, had much shorter tenure as towns.

Silverton acquired both post office and newspaper in 1875, and the town began to take on an air of permanence despite the fact that the railroad's arrival was still seven years away.

The town's establishment was accompanied by a progression from placer mining to lode mining— seeking ore in the veins within bedrock of the mountains. While one or two gold properties were pursued in this manner, the majority of the properties worked in the mid-1870s were dealing with a heretofore cursed darker metal—silver. Both silver and gold were recognized as the basis for currency at that time, and the new camp in the rugged San Juans carried its own weight in a short time, significantly enough to attract the interest of the Denver & Rio Grande, which ultimately completed its branch line through Durango to Silverton in July, 1882.

The prospector and his pack animal continued to find a place in the rugged San Juans, as one canyon after another was explored for mineral potential. But when a worthy prospect was found, a claim would likely change hands—giving the prospector a financial reward for his labors and placing a capitalist with more sophisticated methods and personnel in charge of the property. Proven ore reserves often resulted in the erection of a mill to concentrate the ores, although many richer operations simply hand-sorted the broken rock that was richest, and shipped it in that form. This was particularly true before the railroad arrived, but the practice continued into this century from more remote mining claims.

Ore that is either rich enough in its basic form, or concentrated through the milling process, is next processed and refined through a smelting operation, and there were a number of early attempts to operate the all-important smelters in the high San Juans during the early years. But since this process is fire-oriented, it is usually inefficient at higher elevations, and all of the smelting attempts at or near Silverton were relatively short-lived—from the first, hauled over Stony Pass in wagons, to one of the last, which was a project of famed Hope Diamond owner Thomas Walsh.

The railroad, ironically, played a role in the absence of smelters in Silverton when it purchased

The Old Hundred mill in Cunningham Gulch was located at one of the more massive mine operation sites near Silverton. Many factors (property tax policies not the least among them) have resulted in the loss of many of these historic structures, some of which were torn down or burned on the site. This photograph shows the Old Hundred as it appeared in 1960. Today it is gone.

These three views look toward Kendall Mountain which rises to an elevation of 13,066' behind Silverton. These mid-winter photographs show well the variety of architecture seen in the structures which exist in Silverton. On the opposite page we can see the elegant United Church building in Silverton, and a prominent frame home of the mining era.

Dell A. McCoy Photographs

The Grand Imperial Hotel is probably the most widely known, and best remembered of all the buildings seen in Silverton. It has recently undergone (and continues to undergo) extensive 1880s style refurbishing under the care and attention of its current owners, Ken and Mary Helen Marlin. The view of Greene Street above was made in 1979. Since that time the structure four doors above the Grand Imperial caved in from snow load and has been replaced by a two-story compatible structure. Note the community Christmas tree in the street at right.

Dell A. McCoy Photographs

the remains of the first one and moved the vital parts to Durango, which remained the vicinity's main smelting center for years.

As with virtually all mining camps, early crude log construction was soon replaced with substantial frame structures. Some existing Silverton homes and business houses can be traced to 1870s origins, and still more to the ornate pseudo-Victorian building boom of the 1880s.

Even though the railroad's exact arrival date was open to speculation, the certainty of rail connection with the outside world spurred development, and the

community's first commercial brick building was erected in 1879, the first stone a year later.

With the newspaper—which continues to this date as the oldest continuously operated business on Colorado's Western Slope—as a cornerstone, Silverton's economic community grew. A bank opened in 1880—in fact, two of them. Mercantile and outfitting stores thrived, bringing their goods over the difficult and time-consuming pass routes until the train would drastically improve the import situation in 1882.

Religious services were conducted in a variety of

June 6, 1978 was the day that locomotive Number 476 "split" the switch on the last curve before the end of track in Silverton. 476 was at the head of the second section of the passenger train, the first section of which was pulled by Number 473. D&RGW workers discuss the mishap as then San Juan County Sheriff, the late Virgil Mason looks on. As seen in the photo below, locomotive Number 478 arrived from Durango at 5:30 P.M., and attempted to tug her sister off the turnout without success. Rerailing efforts lasted throughout the night, with train service resuming the next day. Another, more significant, mishap occurred two days earlier with the cave in of the thin roof of a mining area under Lake Emma at the Sunnyside mine, with the result that Lake Emma washed down through the mine, and out the portal of the American Tunnel several thousand feet below doing a tremendous amount of damage to the mine in the process. Although this accident caused a long period of cleaning up and rebuilding at the mine (Silverton's largest single employer at the time), no one was hurt. Miraculously, the cave in occurred on a Sunday night when no miners were working. The photographer took advantage of the warm evening to hike partway up Anvil Mountain for this unusual, and rare panorama. Significantly, all of the D&RGW's existing motive power on the branch was in Silverton at the time, and recorded in this series of photographs.

Dell A. McCoy Photographs

The house known now as The Wingate House is an excellent example of modern day restoration. The home, owned and restored by Fritz Klinke and Loren Lew, today serves as a bed-and-breakfast establishment. Three interested Silvertonians (from left to right, Fritz Klinke, Bill Jones and Allen Nossaman) were making an inspection as work progressed. On the opposite page are two views of another Fritz Klinke restoration project, his current home on Reese Street. Another pair of Reese Street properties are shown in the center. Two more interesting Silverton buildings are seen below; the "Tower House," and the now beautifully renovated "Alma House," owned by Don and Jolene Stott. The Alma House no longer sports a false front, and has undergone extensive exterior and interior remodeling.

Another carefully maintained and preserved Silverton structure, the home built by pioneer merchant George Bausman, witnessed stagecoach traffic through the tourist season of 1979. Below, in 1971, an earlier stagecoach passed by the beautiful Masonic Hall. In the photograph above and to the right, the interior of a newly constructed building, Smedleys Ice Cream Parlor, demonstrates a successful attempt by its owners to recreate an historically appropriate building upon what had been an empty lot on Greene Street. This building, another Klinke-Lew project, is thought by most Silverton visitors to be one of the existing older buildings. Few perceive its modern genesis. Below, another interior is seen. This is the dining room and bar of the popular and justly famous Bent Elbow on "Notorious Blair Street."

Dell A. McCoy Photographs

The Wyman Building, on Greene Street, constructed with native stone, as it appeared in 1967.

locations, but the relative isolation meant few men of the cloth found their way to Silverton, fewer stayed any length of time, and even fewer founded viable churches. Only the Catholic and Congregational (now United Church) churches can trace beginnings to before the turn of the century in Silverton. The Congregational church structure has been identified as the second oldest church structure in Western Colorado, and the third oldest church of that denomination in the state.

An all-purpose, cabin-like structure served as the first school, center of worship, and town board meeting site. It was typical in the earlier years that pupils would attend the elementary grades, but—with all family members needed in a given enterprise to make it work—it was rare for a student to remain enrolled through high school. Thus, it wasn't until 1884, that a debate over whether a new school was needed was finally resolved, and until 1885 that an impressive new frame building was occupied.

As the 1890s approached, Silverton prospered relative to the early years. A variety of metals kept the camp going, but silver was still the mainstay, and the repeal of the Sherman Silver Purchase Act in 1893 set Silverton back, just as it did a number of other mining towns in Colorado.

Faith in the long-term viability of the mines gave the community a will to live, however, and mining continued on a number of fronts—balancing what was left of the silver market with continuing production in gold and base metals. Many of the town's finer residences were constructed during this period—a majority of them surviving today as fine examples of the varied architectural styles which characterized home construction during that period.

The price of silver had fallen from $1.29 per ounce to 40 cents per ounce in the 1893 silver panic, but

during the dozen years before 1900, three more narrow gauge railroad lines were constructed to connect Silverton with mining producers up each of the three major mountain canyons leading into the town from higher elevations. These rail lines made continuing production and haulage feasible from a number of mines in the area—first the Yankee Girl, Guston, Vanderbilt and others in the Red Mountain area, and later the Silver Lake, Iowa, Royal Tiger, Sunnyside and Gold King. The resultant stability was enough to see Silverton through and set the stage for the town's finest hour after the turn of the century.

Of the three railroads, the Silverton Railroad—the oldest—went to the Red Mountain District north of Silverton, and served the short-lived camps of Chattanooga, Red Mountain, Ironton and Albany. The Silverton Northern Railroad—the most profitable over the longest period of time—went straight up the Animas River from Silverton, serving Howardsville and Eureka well into the 20th century and running up into Animas Forks for a few years. A branch from this line also served the Green Mountain Mill up Cunningham Gulch for a time.

The third railroad was named the Silverton, Gladstone & Northerly. Despite its pretentious name, it simply linked Silverton with the Gold King Mill at the small mining town of Gladstone up Cement Creek. Built by the Gold King company, it was eventually acquired by the interests of Otto Mears, who had constructed the other two lines and who had built many of the vicinity's early toll roads, earning for himself the title "Pathfinder of the San Juans."

For all practical purposes, the Silverton Railroad was abandoned in 1921, the Silverton, Gladstone & Northerly in 1937 and the Silverton Northern in 1942, although regular traffic on each line ceased a

Greene Street, and the former site of a popular melodrama—the San Juan Bar.

number of years prior to the respective abandonment dates. Some traces of each of the little lines remain, particularly in the way of cut-and-fill grades and bridge abutments.

Weathering the Silver Panic of 1893 did indeed point the durable mining town and county seat of San Juan County toward what was perhaps its finest decade as the 20th century opened.

Silverton's two banks dated from earlier days, and the Silverton Brewery had become a well-established purveyor of locally brewed beer. It was by then in impressive stone quarters at the southern edge of town.

Three churches—Congregational, Episcopal and Catholic—were consistently serving the religious needs of the community, the latter from a proud new brick edifice. All three buildings still stand, the Episcopal church having become a Baptist mission facility.

A few brick structures had been built just before the turn of the century, notable among them the Benson Hotel, the Bausman Building and the Chicago Saloon, all still standing. But a new century brought a euphoric atmosphere to Silverton, and many of the public buildings were erected during this period.

The Miners' Union Hall, which has housed a variety of lodges and union organizations through the years and is currently the home of the local American Legion post, was erected in the year 1901, as was an impressive matched pair of stone commercial buildings on Greene Street constructed by early merchants Fritz Hoffman and Billy Cole, who were good friends and originally had their names atop their respective buildings.

In 1902, San Juan County constructed its brick jail building on what was to become the courthouse

The Laundromat on Greene Street was also photographed in 1967.

The Silverton Hardware on Greene Street was photographed in 1967.

square. The distinctive jail building now houses the museum of the San Juan County Historical Society, which is open from Memorial Day through mid-October and which contains numerous diverse artifacts from the county's history.

The year 1902 also saw construction of the Wyman Building, first of two major buildings to be built with a locally quarried red sandstone, from which the Silverton Town Hall was also later constructed—right across the street. The Wyman Building features a hand-carved pack burro on the building's nameplate over the corner, reportedly carved by Louis Wyman, early-day teamster who built the structure.

A long campaign to erect a public library with funds from Andrew Carnegie was culminated in 1906 when the Silverton Public Library opened its doors to the community. An architectural classic, the building serves the same purpose today.

A year later, the impressive San Juan County Courthouse was completed on courthouse square, in front of the 1902 jail. The building has served as the seat of county government since its occupation in 1907, and is an outstanding example of public building architecture from the period. Mosaic tiles adorn the hallway floors, and woodwork and moldings are unaltered from the original.

The Miners' Union Hospital, which housed medical facilities and clinical operations up into the 1970s and is now the office building for the community's largest mining operation, was erected in 1907 as well. It is located on the site of the first cabin built in the original town limits of Silverton by Francis Marion Snowden, the only one of Silverton's founding fathers who continued to live in Silverton after the turn of the century.

This is the General Store and Candle Shop on Blair Street which is operated year round by Ruth Ward, a long-time Silvertonian, who is also the county nurse.

The photo below depicts the early use of pressed steel ornamentation over frame construction on a Blair Street establishment.

Dell A. McCoy Photograph

This scene is the view to the south, across town, toward the canyon of the Animas River. It is through this canyon that the railroad comes to Silverton.

This store building on Blair Street is known to locals as the "North Pole," from its days as a saloon of the same name.

The Silverton Town Hall—second of the public structures utilizing the red sandstone of local origin—was finished in 1908, and is still the seat of the municipal government today. More mosaic tile and a striking rotunda are features of this building, which houses a recently restored assembly room for community programs and functions. While under construction, the front wall of the town hall fell into the street one day, and the contractor who had successfully completed the county courthouse had to complete the city's project.

The last major public building of this period was the present brick school, erected in 1911. Upon its completion, a huge but hazardous frame structure was demolished; it had served as the school since 1886, with additions appended along the way.

This period of relative affluence was followed by harder times, and it is notable that virtually no major construction took place in Silverton for the next 50 years—a fact that has singularly given the town much of its character as a period mining town.

Within the past two decades, some new construction has taken place, but it has wisely blended with the older architecture in the commercial and public building sectors of the town. The ongoing debate over imitative architecture continues, even in Silverton, but to date, nothing oppressive has been attempted and many pleasing options have been exercised.

During what many feel was the apex of its existence during the first decade of this century, Silverton became one of the first towns of its size in the country to own its own water, sewer and electrical systems. The water system was privately

owned until 1901, and the coal-fired power generating system was in private hands until around 1903. Municipal operation of water and sewer systems continues, but the experiment with municipally owned power generation facilities ended in 1907 when electricity was purchased from the regional supplier.

It was also during this period that San Juan County reached its peak population of nearly 5,000. Census counts were challenging, for the figure included not only those living and working in Silverton or the other mountain communities which survived beyond 1900, but literally hundreds of men who lived primarily in boarding houses scattered among the cliffs and crags of the San Juan Mountains. These miners, often immigrants and usually single, would frequently be scheduled to spend work periods of up to ten days at the mine site, then leave the confines of the boarding house for an extended "weekend" of three or four days in Silverton.

A number of these boarding houses remain in various stages of decay. One of the classics is that of the Old Hundred upper levels, perched high on the barren face of Galena Mountain east of Howardsville.

Silverton did not experience the extensive fires which characteristically leveled block after block in Colorado mining camps like Cripple Creek, Creede or Leadville—another reason so many 19th Century buildings remain in use today in the colorful town on the Animas River. Silverton's worst single disaster was of another kind—a devastating outbreak of Spanish Influenza that centered its entry into the town around the celebrations of armistice in 1918.

Public buildings were closed, mail was fumigated and residents were warned to stay home. But Silverton's isolation still did not protect it from the flu epidemic. Forty-two persons reportedly died during the first week of the outbreak, and the town hall doubled as hospital space as numbers of the stricken mounted. Coffins were hastily constructed for the dying, but the numbers ultimately outstripped the carpenters' efforts, and many victims were buried in common trenches in the Silverton cemetery. When it was all over, a revised listing indicated the flu had killed 146 people in Silverton and vicinity, and more than one family numbered more than one of its members among the fatalities.

Mining delivered its promise to Silverton from earlier decades of prospecting and development as the 20th Century began to age. But the shift began from the smaller, locally managed operations of the camp's first two decades to absentee ownership and control by larger corporations. The Stoibers, who had developed the Silver Lake properties, sold their holdings to the Guggenheim interests in 1901. The Sunnyside, which gradually grew from a small to large operation of steady production, ultimately turned Eureka into a company town. When the company pulled the plug on the project in 1938 after decades of mining ore from Lake Emma basin and transporting it by aerial tram to Eureka for milling, it virtually killed Eureka in one blow, and dealt a telling blow to Silverton's economy for many years. The Shenandoah-Dives Mining Company operated a number of Arastra Gulch properties through the years, from the old Silver Lake group to the newer Mayflower. This firm mined marginal properties through times of unfavorable metal prices and kept scores of men employed until finally bowing to the inevitable in 1952, setting the stage for the mid-1950s depression that was really Silverton's most challenging time.

It was a time when most of America was demolishing and modernizing. But Silverton, ironically, was unable to afford to do so, and the result—most would agree—provided a happy consequence for a later diversification of the economy.

While mining lagged in the 1940s and 1950s, another phenomenon was at work: Silverton was being discovered as a scenic, recreational and historic spot by an increasingly mobile society finally able to reach the area on its own terms—the family car.

One element in that discovery resulted in Silverton and the surrounding country finding use as a backdrop for a number of motion pictures. The relatively unspoiled town, the surviving narrow gauge railroad and spectacular mountain scenery gave the makers of Hollywood Westerns a variety of natural sets to choose from, and the area starred proudly in such movies of the era as "Run for Cover," "Ticket to Tomahawk," "Maverick Queen," "Great Day in the Morning" and "Across the Wide Missouri."

Another element was the revival of the Denver & Rio Grande Western's narrow gauge Silverton branch as a tourist attraction. While winter operations were curtailed in the 1950s as a reflection of mine closures, service was never suspended, and increasing numbers of railroad fans and tourists looking for something unique began riding behind the steam-powered, coal-fired locomotives up the marvelously engineered grade from Durango into Silverton. The Denver & Rio Grande Western had its sights set on abandoning the line—as it had many of its other branch lines in Colorado—but a couple of outspoken train conductors began espousing the logic of keeping a picturesque, historic, awe-inspiring line in operation. Traffic over the line grew steadily year after year and Silverton staunchly vowed to stand behind saving the railroad which had been its literal artery for 70 years.

The railroad company attempted twice to abandon the line, but Silverton's determination and the still-increasing use of the route resulted in denial of abandonment petitions by the Public Utilities Commission. Ridership increased as the notoriety of the railroad spread, and—coupled with increasing automobile traffic—thrust Silverton into the role of courting both mining and tourism.

Debates over the impact of each industry grew in intensity year after year, but a myriad of factors at work in society as a whole—including inflation and

emphasis on centralization and mobility—convinced Silverton that it needed to make the best of each situation in order to survive in an era when other towns of its size were literally disappearing in droves.

Frustrated in its attempts to abandon a popular branch line, the Denver & Rio Grande Western ultimately obtained permission to sell the branch, which resulted in the acquisition of the 45-mile section between Durango and Silverton in 1981 by the present owner, Charles Bradshaw Jr., operating as the Durango & Silverton Narrow Gauge Railroad Company. The line's popularity continues, and during the height of the summer season in 1986, four trains operated daily into Silverton.

Mining's low ebb ended as the 1960s opened. A striking shrine overlooking the town from Anvil Mountain had been constructed in the late 1950s as an expression of faith despite the dismal times. Christened "Christ of the Mines" by the Silvertonians who erected it, the shrine features a figure of Christ, carved from Italian marble, shielded by a grotto constructed of stone from the old Silverton Brewery. Within a year after its erection, initiaion of the present era's largest mining project in the area was announced by Standard Uranium, later Standard Metals Corporation. The company reopened the old workings at and near the Sunnyside veins, but reached them this time through an extension of the old American Tunnel or Gold King Tunnel at Gladstone. Employment levels stabilized in a few years, and when the $35 per ounce ceiling on the price of gold was lifted, the company coincidentally encountered increasingly rich gold ores, bringing realization to a dream that would have made many old timers smile with pride at their faith in the San

This barn and stable building—dating to the 1880s—stood on 13th Street near Cement Creek, but was torn down after a roof cave in due to heavy snow.

Juans and in Silverton.

How the same company can go bankrupt twice in a dozen years mining gold is another story entirely, but it hinges on the fact that the swing of the pendulum to absentee ownership and management—started around the turn of the century—had finally been realized. Silverton may be the seat of the resource, but its destiny as a mining town has most recently been decided in the New York board room and the Denver bankruptcy court. Surviving the second bankruptcy, the old Sunnyside project is still operating, now owned by Sunnyside Gold, a subsidiary of Echo Bay Mining Company.

Silverton's tenacity has literally become one of its trademarks, yet its somewhat hackneyed nickname as "The Town That Wouldn't Quit" has seemed to gain in significance as the years have passed. It has survived attempts to consolidate its school with other districts which appear close only on the misleading markings of a two-dimensional map. It has survived attempts to consolidate its county government with neighbors who already view it as some distant,

In 1978, when this photograph was made, train passengers enjoyed this view of Silverton near the end of track. Sultan Mountain dominates the view to the southwest, beautifully clothed in autumn gold.

Dell A. McCoy Photograph

mythical mountain kingdom with which they have little in common.

It has survived the vagaries of the mining industry —a community which testifies to the fact that a literal sense of community can outlast and outlive the best mining promotions, and the worst. And anyone who has spent a winter among its snow drifts, and blizzards and sub-zero temperatures knows of another kind of survival that makes summer—however humorously short it may be—very special indeed.

Yet survive it does, this improbable town which, unless you are on a single, narrow railroad right-of-way, can be left only by climbing in elevation regardless of the direction one takes; this improbable town which is older than any of its neighbors in more suitable locations on any side; this improbable town with a legendary fourteen-day growing season; this improbable town where it can snow on the Fourth of July.

But then Silverton's strength comes from the caliber of its challenges ... and lots of experience.

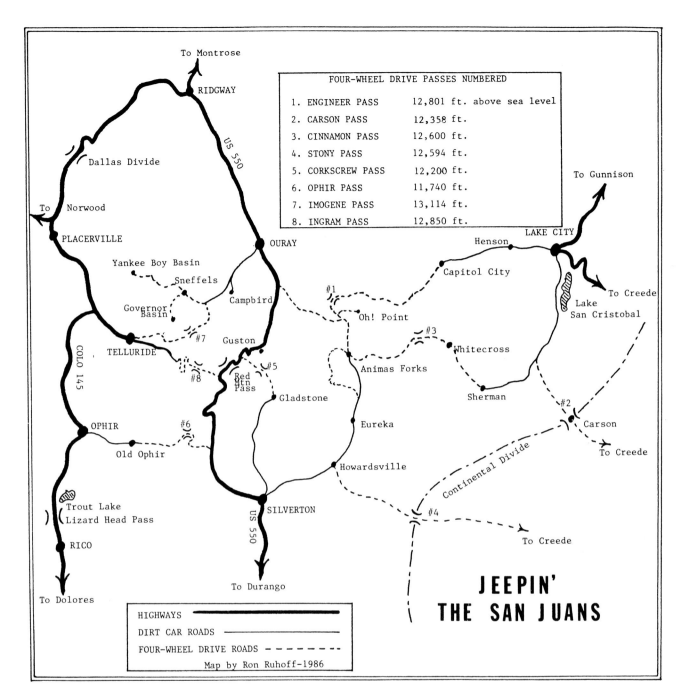

JEEPIN'
THE SAN JUANS

HIGHWAYS
DIRT CAR ROADS
FOUR-WHEEL DRIVE ROADS
Map by Ron Ruhoff-1986

As you approach the San Juan Mountains from the north, on U.S. Highway 550, heading toward Ouray from Montrose, you know immediately that you're headed for very special country. Looming ever-closer ahead are the jagged summits of Precipice and Coxcomb Peaks and the entire Sneffels Massif viewed across the beautiful Dallas Valley. The mountains of the great San Juan Range are more precipitous, colorful and snow-filled than any other range in Colorado. In the center of this mountain-scape panorama you see the pyramid shaped Mount Abrams directly ahead as the highway guides you through a narrow canyon alongside the Uncompahgre River. Soon the canyon opens up into a Shangri-La like valley which is occupied by the little town of Ouray. The town takes its name from the famous Ute Indian chief and is completely surrounded by the towering peaks of the San Juans. Signs announce that you are in the "Switzerland of America" and that Ouray is, indeed, the "Jeep Capital of the World."

Jeepin' The San Juans
by Ron Ruhoff

The Author's Jeep is parked atop the 13,000' crest of the Engineer Pass road.
Beyond the jeep, to the west, we can see the Sneffels massif dominated in this
view by Mount Potosi.

From Ouray, Highway 550 takes on the name "Million-Dollar Highway" as it winds through seemingly impossible canyons toward Red Mountain Pass and the cities of Silverton and Durango. If that isn't thrilling enough for you, Ouray is also the jumping-off place for the greatest concentration of high, four-wheel-drive roads to be found anywhere in the country. Passes with names like Engineer, Imogene, Corkscrew and Cinnamon cross high ridges exceeding 13,000 feet in elevation, inter-connecting Ouray, Silverton, Lake City and Telluride with narrow, steep, rocky roads far too difficult for ordinary passenger cars. For this reason, modern mechanical burros such as Jeeps, Scouts, Broncos, Blazers and numerous other brand-names are the way to negotiate much of this San Juan back-country. If you don't have such a vehicle of your own, there are several opportunities to locally rent a jeep or join one of the guided 4WD tours available in Ouray.

With the accompanying map as a guide, I'd like to take you now over several of the most famous and awesome 4WD passes. Since this type of recreation developed after World War II as a result of the military "jeep", the term "jeeping" still sticks, no matter what kind of vehicle you might be driving. As we follow these fascinating roads, I'll attempt to fill in some history, information on driving technique and excerpts from my own adventures over the past 30 years since I drove my first jeep, a 1942 Ford military, through this country in 1957.

Engineer Pass

Even today, with many fascinating jeep roads to follow throughout the San Juans, Engineer Pass remains one of the oldest and most beautiful. From Ouray, we head up the beginnings of the Million Dollar Highway toward Red Mountain Pass.

One particular journey, about three years ago, found my family in our Bronco, and friends from Illinois using a rented Scout. Our group of twelve stopped first at the Bear Creek Falls turnout to view the tremendous cascade that tumbles beneath the highway and to look at the historical marker that commemorates Otto Mears, early-day "Pathfinder of the San Juans." Mears was the original builder of this highway when it was a scary toll wagon road in the 1880s. Today's modern, paved highway is a far cry from the original toll-road, but still quite an exciting undertaking for those not used to mountain

131

In the photograph to the left, the author sits on the hood of his Bronco which is perched on "Oh! Point," one of the most spectacular spots to which one can drive a vehicle. This point is on a short side road off Engineer Pass above Ouray. 14,017′ Wetterhorn Peak is in the distance.

As evidenced by the depth of the snow, this is a photograph of an early season crossing of Engineer Pass. The trip was made in mid-June shortly after the pass was opened. Often, many San Juan passes are not open by this date. The Ghost town of Carson, seen below, is located on the Continental Divide at 12,300′. This photo, made in 1957, shows the structures which remained at that time, the remnants of Christopher J. Carson's Bonanza King Mine. The author's partner, Bill Hedges, views the townsite from the old 1942 military jeep.

Ron Ruhoff Photographs

driving. I reflected on the fact that we were following in Mears' foot-steps almost exactly 100 years after the opening of his tollgate and 25 years since I first drove a jeep up this canyon and over Engineer Pass. In the intervening years, I have driven this and other San Juan passes countless times, but never tire of it and especially enjoy the opportunity to take guests along for their first ride.

A short distance above Bear Creek Falls, the canyon splits to either side of Mount Abrams. The right-hand canyon is the Million-Dollar Highway (named for its high cost of construction in the 1940s) which follows Red Mountain Creek. We follow the Uncompahgre River itself to the left, first making a

stop, just off the pavement, to lock in the front-wheel hubs of our vehicles for the rough climb ahead.

The name "Uncompahgre", which is given to the river, national forest, plateau and a mountain peak, is a Ute word which translates to "hot-water-springs." It was given to the little valley now occupied by the town of Ouray because of the natural springs that flow there. Today the never-ending source of hot water is used to feed a beautiful million-gallon swimming pool, one of Ouray's most popular attractions.

Our jeep road follows the Uncompahgre through a narrow canyon of deep gorges and waterfalls on its way to timberline where the terrain opens up into a

Ron Ruhoff Photograph

The Lee Mansion was still standing when the author first visited Capital City in 1957. George Lee had hopes that his town would become the capital of Colorado, and planned for the Governor to live in this large brick house. The house is no longer standing.

large alpine plateau where we see evidence of the tremendous mining activity of bygone days. The town of Mineral Point was once located near the fork in the road which allows one to travel either to Silverton or Lake City. These roads were also the original handiwork of Otto Mears, dating back to the 1880s. We're headed for Engineer Pass itself and follow the left fork. The rocky road makes numerous switchbacks along the southern face of Engineer Mountain now as we head toward the 13,000 foot pass. On the way up, we pass other vehicles, on occasion, also enjoying this favorite among San Juan passes. At times we see one of the red tour jeeps from Ouray with its many passengers showing happy faces, but still clinging to hats and stomachs, as we somehow pass each other at spots seemingly too narrow to do so. With friendly waves to each other, we continue on.

On the way up Engineer, there is a side road that is an absolute must, especially if you have passengers who are making their first mountain jeep trip, as ours were this time. About half-way between the Silverton turnoff and the pass, we go straight ahead from the east end of a switchback and drive toward a saddle on the east ridge of Engineer Mountain. The road appears tame enough at first, but as we approach an obvious drop-off, the tracks turn right and up a steep grade toward a rocky cliff. Our passengers eyes began to widen as their non-chalant driver casually eased the Bronco out to the edge of the cliff an inch at a time in "granny" gear to a final stop. Through the windshield we could see nothing but blue sky and the distant jagged summits of the San Juans. I said, "OK folks, let's get out and have a look."

Our friends Dennis and his wife, Joy, were the first to get out. Having never been to this part of Colorado, they looked a bit startled. Joy took one frightened look at our precarous parking place and immediately sat down on the ground, exclaiming, "Ohhhhhh!"

A first ride to a place like this can affect people in many different ways, but Joy's exclamation was typical of most who are not used to high mountain country. That's why this spot has un-officially been called "OH! Point" for over thirty years since early jeep tour guides first coined the phrase.

From our vantage point the cliff drops abruptly away a thousand feet just inches in front of the Bronco's wheels and ahead we see a vast expanse of colorful San Juan mountains and valleys. From left to right, the view shows Coxcomb Peak—13,660 ft, Wetterhorn Peak—14,017 ft., the Little Matterhorn and Uncompahgre Peak which, at 14,309 feet high is the tallest in the San Juan Range and sixth highest in Colorado. In the valley below, a narrow, winding ribbon marks the Engineer road following Henson Creek toward Lake City. We're in sheep grazing country and we can faintly hear their bleating voices floating up from the vast flocks seen grazing the alpine meadows far below. Yes, this is "OH/ Point", one of the most spectacular places one may drive a four-wheeler to in the entire country.

Time now to head back to the main road and the pass itself. After the switchbacks are accomplished, a long, narrow track in the talus slope takes us to the top. The road tops out at an even 13,000 feet just below the 13,190 ft. summit of Engineer Mountain, even though the actual pass is beyond, around the corner at a slightly lower elevation. From this vantage point we see a wonderful panorama of the San Juan ranges. To the west, 14,150 foot Mount Sneffels and 13,786 foot Mount Potosi dominate the scene above Ouray, while to the south, the "Needles" rise above the Animas River Canyon, Far to the north, the dark, flat-topped bulk of Grand Mesa is plainly visible near Grand Junction. A short side road leads out to the west, to a fine vantage point atop a knoll where you will see an extremely steep road leading up the ridge toward the summit of

Engineer itself. This road actually goes around the peak, just below the summit, and meets up with the Oh Point road. I don't recommend trying it unless you are sure of your vehicle's power and your own driving ability. One can get into serious trouble on such a road if a stall makes it necessary to back down again. I drove it once many years ago in my jeep with no trouble, but I'd hate to have to hit the brakes part way up and attempt it backwards.

We make another stop when we get to the actual Engineer Pass—the divide between Uncompahgre and Gunnison watersheds. The sign indicates our elevation as 12,801 feet and the dominant view is that of the Eagles Nest, a beautiful mountain with a large stain of reddish iron on its side. From here, the road takes us across American Flats where much mineral production once took place. One example was the large Frank Hough Mine which opened in 1881.

As we drive on down the headwaters of Henson Creek, numerous reminders of past mining activity are found. An old stone dynamite hut still stands near the road. Various mills, cabins and a shack with compressor and hoist machinery still inside are also seen. Many beautiful waterfalls enhance the landscape and a worthwhile stop can be made to walk a marked trail to a large waterfall which is not visible from the road.

Parts of Rose's Cabin are still standing where Corydon Rose built a stagecoach stop complete with hotel, bar and livery stable in 1874. Farther down the canyon, you will see a tremendous brick smelter stack still standing across the stream.

Where Matterhorn Creek flows into Henson, we find the few remains of the ghost town of Capitol City, a town which sprang up in the 1870s with the discovery of silver. A resident by the name of George Lee was so confident his town would become the capital of Colorado, he built a huge brick mansion which was to be the governor's home. The structure cost him one dollar per brick as the materials were hauled in from Pueblo. Today all traces of the home have disappeared. A new house was just recently constructed on the same spot. Only one original building remains in Capitol City today—an old cabin, which has suffered unfortunate vandalism to its front log wall.

We've been on a good automobile road for some time now as we go on through the old town of Henson where the Ute-Ulay Mine once operated. Look for another very beautiful waterfall on Henson Creek not far off the road to the right. The final stretch of Henson Creek takes us through close-in walls of conglomerate rock as we approach Lake City. Engineer Pass has been a grand experience for scenic views and ghost town exploring, but is, by no means, the difficult road it once was in the earlier days of jeeping. Continued use and county maintenance have tamed the road so that even smaller 2-wheel drive cars can negotiate it in late summer and fall when the terrain is drier.

Lake City is the seat of Hinsdale County and occupies a beautiful little valley along the Lake Fork of the Gunnison River. The name is derived from nearby Lake San Cristobal, which is second only to Grand Lake as the largest natural lake in Colorado. From here paved highways go north to Gunnison or out over Slumgullion Pass to Creede. We intend to "keep on jeepin'" however, so will first head south to Lake San Cristobal. Following the Lake Fork road past the lake, we're now headed for Cinnamon Pass.

Carson and Cinnamon Passes

Before crossing Cinnamon, however, a side trip to the ghost town of Carson is a must. We turn left off the main road about six miles south of the lake and follow a rough, 4WD road up Wager Gulch, five miles to the Carson townsite. Carson had the unique distinction of being built in two sections, one on each side of the continental divide.

The first group of structures you see are the remains of the second city of Carson, built around the gold discoveries of 1896. As you drive on over the divide on Carson Pass, you find the original townsite which was begun in 1881 by a man named Christopher J. Carson. (Not to be confused with Kit Carson). His Bonanza King Mine produced silver until the crash of 1893. Carson nearly became a ghost town then, but the new gold discoveries at the Bachelor Mine in Wager Gulch three years later got things going again. Today several cabins, a boarding house and stable remain in lower Carson. There are also a number of original buildings at the upper townsite which is located at well over 12,000 feet in elevation. Their windblown condition is a good indication of the severe weather encountered up here. The road goes through upper Carson and on down Lost Trail Creek, eventually coming out near Creede. Friends of mine drove this a number of years ago, but I have not tried it myself and would hesitate to say one could make it.

Taking up our original course out of Lake City, we now return to the Lake Fork road and head for Cinnamon Pass. This road, like Engineer Pass, has been tamed over the years since I first drove it in 1958. Along the way, stops at the ghost towns of Sherman and Whitecross are worthwhile, although little remains at either townsite. The Black Wonder Mine was the source of employment in Sherman and the Tobasco Mine and Mill were located at Whitecross. Whitecross was named for a unique natural white quartz formation in the shape of a cross. If you look carefully near the top of a mountain peak, directly across the valley from the road, you can see the white X among the darker rocks.

A few more switchbacks take us easily to the top of 12,600 foot Cinnamon Pass. The name was derived from nearby Cinnamon Mountain, which was named for the cinnamon colored rocky terrain in this area. The road offers no great difficulties as it heads down into the Animas canyon, coming out at the town of Animas Forks. At the townsite we meet the branch road to Mineral Point and Engineer Pass.

The ghost town of Animas Forks appears much the same today as it did in this 1957 photo. The old military jeep is parked at the junction of the roads which lead to Engineer and Cinnamon Passes, and the road down to Silverton.

Animas Forks remains a large ghost town today with many cabins and mine structures. The town was extremely busy in its day, being the center of mining activity for many miles around. Two smelters once operated here and a narrow gauge railroad called the Silverton Northern was built in 1904 by Otto Mears to haul the large volume of ore down to Silverton. The railroad continued to operate until 1942.

The so-called "Walsh House" remains in the Forks today as one of Colorado's most often pictured ghost town buildings. This once-beautiful home with the bay window facing across the valley is easily recognized. The family of Tom Walsh, of Campbird Mine fame, supposedly lived in this home. Preservation work has been done on this house in recent years with help from the San Juan County Historical Society and the Ghost Town Club of Colorado.

From Animas Forks, several 4WD roads may be driven by following **California Gulch**. One goes to Lake Como and another **circles Picayune Gulch** and meets the main **Animas road halfway** between Animas Forks and Eureka.

On the way down to **Silverton**, we pass through Eureka, where the large **concrete foundations** of the Sunnyside Mill are seen. Another four miles brings us to Howardsville and the turnoff to Stony Pass.

Stony Pass

The Stony Pass road follows Cunningham Gulch past fascinating abandoned aerial tramways to the top of the 12,594 foot pass. The views from the top aren't particularly spectacular, but if you take the time to hike southwest to the top of a small hill, a breathtaking view of the entire Weminuche Wilderness Area and the Needle Mountains is available. The road then leads on down to the Rio Grande headwaters toward Creede. During wet weather and early summer some boggy conditions may be encountered on the east side. The side road to Kite Lake and the ghost town of Beartown is now closed to vehicular travel, but a hike to the townsite is worthwhile to see the remaining structures and the Sylvanite Mine.

Continuing back on the Animas River road, Silverton is the next stop before beginning the next leg of our 4WD journey. With so much written about this town, famous today for the Durango & Silverton Narrow Gauge Railroad, we will continue on.

Corkscrew Pass

We'll now head straight north out of Silverton, along the grade of the Silverton, Gladstone &

Northerly Railroad, another Mears line, to the ghost town of Gladstone. Practically nothing remains of the old town except the large foundations of the Gold King Mill, which produced some 8 million dollars in its day. Much present-day mining activity is currently taking place and I suggest caution due to possibly heavy truck traffic along this Cement Creek road.

A number of interesting roads lead out of Gladstone, but our destination is the unique and beautiful Corkscrew Pass. The road climbs to a saddle between Red Mountains Nos. 1 and 2 and offers spectacular views of the brilliant red talus slopes dropping away toward the Million Dollar Highway. The name is derived from Corkscrew Gulch, on the west side of the pass, where the old Silverton Railroad had a covered turntable at the end of a branch line. Corkscrew Pass is truly one of the most colorful places one can visit in the San Juans.

Our road leads out to the old town of Guston near the Million Dollar Highway and Red Mountain Pass. Tremendous mineralization in this area produced riches from mines like the Guston, Yankee Girl and, in more recent years, the Idarado Tunnel, which goes through the mountains to Telluride.

We are once again on U.S. Highway 550 and it's time to tackle the three last passes which all cross high ridges between the Telluride and Ouray/Silverton areas. The first will be Ophir Pass.

Ophir Pass

From Red Mountain Pass we head toward Silverton, passing first the turn-off to Ingram Pass—the infamous Black Bear Road—which we will save for last.

Heading south on the highway, we go around the Chattanooga curve and soon turn west at the "Ophir Pass" sign, following the road up the middle fork of Mineral Creek. Ophir Pass offers a relatively easy drive to its 11,740 ft. crest among jumbles of broken rock and talus. Once atop, a fine view of 14,017 ft. Wilson Peak in the San Miguel Range is seen, and below, the little valley where the town of Old Ophir is located. As you drive down around the first switchback, you can see the long stretch of narrow road across the canyon where you will soon be driving on hazardous, loose talus. To the right you can see the remains of the older steep road going directly to the top which was replaced by the switchback in the early 1960s. My first trip over Ophir in 1958 was a memorable one, as we had to go up that steep old

Corkscrew Pass crosses the Red Mountains between Gladstone and the "Million Dollar Highway." The elevation at the top is 12,200', and the views are among the most beautiful to be found in Colorado. Its name is derived from Corkscrew Gulch, on the west side, where the Silverton Railroad had a unique covered turntable.

137

The long talus slope on the west side of Ophir Pass lies above the valley floor, and Old Ophir. This pass was tamed in the 1960s with the construction of a new switchback near the top.

road in reverse gear, using the little military jeep, in order to have sufficient power to make the grade. Early-day wagon rides over this pass during the toll-road era, beginning in 1881, must have been quite an experience.

Today's Ophir Pass is far more negotiable, but care must be taken on the long section of talus, where there is practically no room for passing of other vehicles. Look ahead first to see if anyone is coming up-grade, as the rules of the road state that the person on the uphill grade has the right-of-way. One must be prepared at all times, while four-wheeling, to back up to allow someone to pass. One of the most often asked questions by those not familiar with jeeping is "What do you do when you meet someone on these narrow roads"? Easily answered—someone has to back up. Backing up can be difficult and even frightening for those not used to it, but after years of back-country driving, it becomes relatively easy and commonplace. Be courteous and do the backing to a passing spot if it will make it easier for the other opposing driver, even though you may have the right-of-way.

Once down in the valley, we come to the little settlement of Old Ophir. New or just plain "Ophir" is on down the hill at the junction of Colorado Highway 145. Actually New Ophir is older than Old Ophir and Old Ophir is newer than New Ophir! The original town was built in the upper valley in 1878 and was called Howards's Fork after this branch of the San Miguel River. The town eventually took on the biblical name of a source of gold. When Otto Mears built the Rio Grande Southern Railroad around the San Juan Range from Durango to Telluride and Ouray, he laid rails over Lizard Head Pass and on down the San Miguel canyon. In order to negotiate the steep grades below Trout Lake, that railroad was made to cross over itself at the so-called Ophir Loop. The newer settlement sprang up near the rails and most of the people in Old Ophir moved down the hill to the available transportation. In 1953, new mining ventures constructed a series of houses, which are still lived in today in Old Ophir—therefore making it a "newer" town. As you drive through Ophir today, you might want to visit the little post office—certainly one of the tiniest in the entire country. Once on the pavement of Highway 145, we continue on into Telluride.

Telluride

Telluride has made a complete turnaround since my first visit in 1958. Always a mining community, the townspeople tried desperately to bring in more commerce and population during the 1960s to supplement the dwindling mining industry. With the opening of new ski areas, condominiums and hotels, Telluride was "discovered" by the outside world to a greater extent than ever before. Despite present day growing pains and population turnover, Telluride has become one of the most popular recreation and music festival cities in Colorado.

For the four-wheeler, Telluride probably offers more spectacular routes out of its confined valley than any other place in the state. The back roads are too numerous to describe in detail here, but you may eventually want to try the Last Dollar Road to Dallas Divide, Wilson Mesa, Bilk Basin, Bear Creek Falls, the Liberty Bell Mine and others. For this story, we've **saved the two most** scenic and thrilling passes **for the last, Imogene Pass** and Ingram Pass—more commonly **known as the** "Black Bear Road."

Before leaving Telluride, one must visit the San Miguel County Historical Society Museum and talk to Arlene Reid, who has been curator of the museum since its opening over twenty years ago. Arlene and her late husband Homer came to Telluride in 1937 and have been two of the most influential people to live here. I first met Homer in 1962 and did much jeeping with him over the years, learning a lot about the back-roads and history of the area.

Homer Reid was the very first person to buy a jeep in Telluride back in about 1947 when the rugged little vehicles were first made available for civilian use. He surprised the car dealer by paying for it in cash—with a large sack of silver dollars! When he brought it home, many friends and townspeople laughed and said "What're you going to do with that thing?"

Ron Ruhoff Photograph

This rocky lookout is located on the Ouray side of Imogene Pass, the highest drivable pass in the San Juans. Far below, the original Campbird mine workings are seen. Mount Potosi rises in the background near Yankee Boy Basin.

139

The pot of gold at the end of this rainbow is the Idarado Gold Mill at the head of the San Miguel River Canyon in Telluride. Telluride lies on the path of more jeep roads than any other town in Colorado.

Ron Ruhoff Photographs

This photograph taken on the Ouray side of 13,114′ Imogene Pass shows the large snowbank which persisted through the summer. The photo was made in mid-August.

The Mountaintop Mine boarding house still stands in Governor Basin, high above Ouray. Mountain Potosi rises in the background. Heavy snows and the gnawing of packrats and Marmots are slowly destroying the structure.

The Campbird Mine workings are seen below from this viewpoint on the Imogene Pass road near its junction with the Yankee Boy Basin road. Canyon Creek Canyon leads toward Ouray in the background.

He had more foresight than most, for they had no idea then what a popular sport four-wheeling would become in this country.

Imogene Pass

We now head for Imogene Pass, which is the highest drivable pass in the San Juan Range and second only to Mosquito Pass, near Leadville, as the highest such continuous pass in the entire Rocky Mountain chain. The road begins behind the museum building and follows a long sloping grade on the north side of the San Miguel Canyon into Savage Basin. This route is also known as the "Tomboy Road." A short distance above town, a left turn would take one to the city water works and eventually up very steep grades to the Liberty Bell

Mine, another very worthwhile drive. Numerous opportunities for fine views of Telluride below are found along the way, especially if a stop is made at the small tunnel which we must drive through. Take the time to get out here at this excellent vantage point to photograph Telluride and the Pandora area at the head of the San Miguel Canyon far below. A wonderful view of 370 ft. high Bridal Veil Falls and the Black Bear Road switchbacks is obtained as well.

Just beyond the tunnel, a large mine structure on the right marks the site of the Smuggler-Union Mine and we can see ahead to the Tomboy workings in Savage Basin as well as the hairline road of Imogene Pass crossing the ridge high above. If you have already visited the museum in Telluride or read some of the books on the history of this area, perhaps you can begin to realize what a vast system of mines, mills, boarding houses and aerial cable trams once covered this rugged area.

A stop at the Tomboy is worthwhile in order to visit the remaining structures and see the vast number of foundations and crumbled buildings. This was a complete city in itself during its heyday and hundreds of people lived and worked here year-round. By all means, if possible, secure a copy of the book **Tomboy Bride** by Harriet Backus for a thrilling account of what life was like in this busy timberline mining camp during the mining era.

From Tomboy to the top of Imogene Pass, four-wheel-drive low-range is a must. This road was opened for jeep travel to the top of the pass in 1964 and on down the other side to Ouray shortly thereafter. Several sharp, steep switchbacks and a long shelf road along iron stained talus slopes bring you out to the top. The elevation here is 13,114 feet.

One interesting drive to Imogene occurred recently with our Illinois friends. Mick Crouch was driving the rented Scout which had an automatic transmission and no low range gears to shift to. It simply would not make the grade above the Tomboy—even in reverse. Since we had no tow chain with us, I decided to hook my winch cable to the front of the Scout and pull it over the pass. Of course, I had to drive backwards in order to do this—all the way to the **top of the pass**. I'll admit having a rather stiff neck **when we got to the top**, but we all got there with no **difficulty**.

The crest **of Imogene** offers fantastic views in all directions. **Looking** west to the San Miguel Range we can see Lizard Head, Mount Wilson, El Diente, Wilson Peak and Lone Cone. To the north, Mount Sneffels and Mount Potosi thrust jagged summits above Canyon Creek near Ouray. Looking up the ridge to the east, a small stone structure is seen which was known as Fort Peabody. During the miners' strikes in 1904, the Colorado State Militia was sent to man this high point by Governor Peabody, hopefully to keep the wrong people on the right side of the pass. A hike to the old fort is worthwhile. When Imogene was opened in 1964, the America Flag once again flew from a pole on Fort Peabody.

Before driving on down into Imogene Basin, a side road just around the corner, east of Fort Peabody, is recommended for fine views of the Red Mountains and Million Dollar Highway below. You can also see the distant Needle Mountains to the southwest and Uncompahgre Peak toward the northeast. A little side road will lead you down to alpine Ptarmigan Lake, plainly visible to the south.

The roughest portion of Imogene is still ahead as

A caravan of "Jeeps" in Ouray is seen preparing to leave the "Jeep Capital of the World" in this photograph.

The city of Telluride gleams below in this sunset scene taken from atop the ''Coonskin'' lift of the Telluride ski area.

Ron Ruhoff Photograph

Twin Falls is one of the photogenic sights along the Yankee Boy Basin Road above Ouray. Located nearby is one of the largest fields of Columbine in Colorado. Nearing the end of the road, on the right, a stop is made to view 12,698' Stony Mountain.

Ron Ruhoff Photographs

we descend along sharp switchbacks and a narrow, cliff-hanging track into the basin where the old Upper Campbird Mine was located. Need for caution in this area is suggested because of the chance of meeting other vehicles coming up from below. Once past the switchbacks, a beautiful drive through a large, colorful alpine flower garden takes us to the valley below. Large fields of Columbine, Indian Paintbrush and other alpine species cover the hillsides during mid-summer. When the road levels out near the Campbird workings, ample parking places are available to enjoy scenery and explore this historic district.

The Campbird was discovered by Tom Walsh and operated with his partner Andy Richardson. Andy's wife's name was Imogene (pronounced eye-moe-gene), hence the name of the basin and pass. Next, a beautiful waterfall is passed and we begin the traverse of a rather rocky and, sometimes, boggy shelf road that leads around the cliff above the present-day Campbird property. A road does lead directly through their center of operations and on to Ouray, but it is usually off-limits to public travel. Once past this difficult section of road, we join the main route from Ouray to Yankee Boy Basin.

Yankee Boy and Governor Basins

Some of the most photogenic portions of the San Juans are located in the Yankee Boy Basin area. Four-wheel drive is required as we head up Canyon Creek through the ghost town of Sneffels, named after the mountain itself. Mount Sneffels is 14,150 ft. high and was named by early Colorado surveyors for the Icelandic Peak of the same name which Jules Verne described in his book **Journey to the Center of the Earth.** The townsite of Sneffels, which still has a few original structures standing, was centered around the large Revenue and Virginius Mines. Stony Mountain's 12,698 foot rocky summit forms a picturesque backdrop to the scene. Nearby, a left fork in the road offers a fascinating jeep trip into Governor Basin, where the old Virginius Mine is located as well as a tremendous boarding house which was used by the workers of the Mountaintop Mine. Following the main road west above Sneffels, we come to Twin Falls and one of the largest fields of Columbine in Colorado. The rugged cliffs of Mount Potosi rise directly above this area on the north side of the canyon. Eventually the road ends, well above timberline, at Wright's Lake. A fine view of Gilpin

146

The old Smuggler Union mine stands in the foreground in this autumn view of Savage Basin, along the road to Imogene Pass above Telluride.

Peak's 13,694 ft. summit may be seen across this incredibly dark blue lake. Mount Sneffels itself is off to the right and, if you have read Jules Verne's book, it's easy to see why the jagged ridges reminded the surveyors of the peak in Iceland. Be cautious of steep, tilted and washed portions of this road above timberline. My last trip, in 1983, found it in far worse condition than when I first drove to Wright's Lake in 1957.

Time now to head back down the canyon, past the Imogene Pass turnoff, to Ouray. Just above the Campbird Mine property, you will be on a spectacular ledge road, cut out of solid rock. This portion of the road, and the rest to Ouray, is all graded roadbed with which small cars have no difficulty.

From Ouray, we once again head back up the Million Dollar Highway to Red Mountain Pass. Just over the crest of the pass, on the right-hand side, we find the beginning of the Black Bear Road. There is no longer a marker sign here to indicate the turn, but several years ago an interesting one did exist which stated:

TELLURIDE—CITY OF GOLD
12 MILES, 2½ HOURS
YOU DON'T HAVE TO BE CRAZY TO DRIVE
THIS ROAD—BUT IT HELPS!
—JEEPS ONLY—

Even though the sign disappeared several years ago, the road remains and is definitely open to Telluride despite the many negative answers you may get from people in Ouray when questioning them about its condition. The Black Bear and Imogene roads are generally not drivable until about mid-July, when snowslides have finally melted away. Ophir, Engineer and Cinnamon are usually plowed open in early June. San Miguel County does maintain the west side of Black Bear however and it's usually in good condition toward late summer. The "Ajax" slide, which runs consistently during winter and early spring, raises havoc with the west-side switchbacks of the Black Bear and makes annual grading a necessity.

Ron Ruhoff Photograph

A number of original buildings remain at the site of the Tomboy Mine in Savage Basin, where, above timberline, a tremendous mining city was once located.

149

Telluride is seen far below in this view from the Black Bear Mine boarding house on the notorious Black Bear Road. This photograph was taken just a few days before this historic structure was destroyed by fire in 1977.

Ron Ruhoff Photograph

From a high vantage point on the Imogene Pass road, this fine view of the three Red Mountains can be obtained. Far below one can see the "Million Dollar Highway," Red Mountain Pass and the ghost towns of Guston and Red Mountain Town. The Corkscrew Pass jeep road can be seen crossing the ridge just to the right of Red Mountain Number 1.

Ron Ruhoff Photograph

Clouds appear close enough to touch at the top of 13,114' Imogene Pass, shown here and in the photo on the next page. Lying between Telluride and Ouray, it is the highest drivable pass in the San Juans, and is second only to Mosquito Pass as the highest continuous drivable road in Colorado. Fort Peabody is located high on the ridge seen behind the Bronco.

Ron Ruhoff Photographs

As we head up the Black Bear Road, we find that the east side is relatively easy and uneventful. A stop just above timberline is recommended, at an obvious turnout, for a wonderful view of the Red Mountains. If you look south from this vantage point, toward Silverton, you can see Bear Mountain, named for a natural formation of tree growth on its north face. The dark trees plainly show the silhouette of a black bear with paws raised. My old friend Harry Wright, of Telluride, always said it looked like a bear eating an icecream cone. Sure enough, it does!

We continue across alpine meadows and a couple of gentle switchbacks to the summit of Ingram Pass. The elevation here is 12,850 feet and fine views of the jagged summit of Mount Sneffels can be seen to the northwest. This road is often mistakenly called "Black Bear Pass", but Ingram is the historically correct name. The name is attributed to J.B. Ingram, discoverer of the Smuggler Mine in July, 1876.

Now the fun begins. This pass, by the way, is generally considered a one-way road from east to west. Although there are usually no signs to indicate

this, it is the safest way to travel and, by far, the most spectacular, especially if it's your first ride. The first section from the pass on down offers little in the way of a view ahead until you round a sharp switchback and come out at the head of Ingram Basin. Suddenly the view below opens wide and Ingram Lake's mirror-like surface dominates the center of the scene. You can see the shelf road ahead, circling the basin. It is possible to take a side road to the site of the Andrus Mine down near the lake. The trail ahead bounces you on broken talus for some distance before coming to the right-hand fork which leads to the old Black Bear Mine, from which the name of the road was derived. Fine views of the San Miguel Valley are seen straight ahead to the west and the city of Telluride is coming into view far below. First-timers begin to wonder, about this time, how we can possibly drive down into that distant valley, as there is obviously a steep cliff ahead. As I said before, this is where the fun begins! Nearing the brink of the canyon, we make two tight switchbacks, then, pulling in close to the stream, start

154

around the most dangerous and hair-raising portion of the road. Before going down this section, it's a good idea to check your brakes, since you have recently driven through water, and be sure to shift into the lowest possible gear of the 4-WD low range. It is always safer to go down steep grades under power rather than use brakes excessively, which can cause fish-tailing. This spot is an appropriate place for the old statement, which the conductors of the Rio Grande Southern supposedly called out as the trains approached the Telluride station, "TO-HELL-YOU-RIDE!" With consistant grading over the years, this road has also been tamed somewhat since I first drove it in 1960. I've driven the "Bear" practically every year since that time, including two midnight rides—one with lights off and full moon lighting the way. It's always a thrill and a downright beautiful experience.

Before descending this steep, curving shelf road, try to be sure no one is coming up toward you. Even though most drive toward Telluride from Red

Mountain Pass, some do it in reverse and would technically have the right-of-way. (I had to stop in the middle of this spot once, in a rainstorm, and back all the way up to let another pass). Once around the shelf, one more sharp hairpin turn takes you to the stopping point next to the old Black Bear stamp mill. There is adequate room here for several vehicles to park and it's a worthwhile stop to calm nerves, take photos and watch other vehicles come down the steep grade. Ingram Falls drops over the cliff here and the first views of Bridal Veil Falls are seen ahead. We're stopped at the spot where the Black Bear boarding house used to stand—directly across the road from the mill. Unfortunately, the building was destroyed by fire in 1977 after some people built a campfire inside on its wooden floors! Evidence of such thoughtless firemaking are found on the floors of many ghost town buildings these days. No wonder so many of our historic buildings are disappearing! In the days of operation, ore from the Black Bear Mine was carried to this mill on aerial cable tram,

The old Black Bear mine boarding house, depicted on this and the following page, is the site of a stop made on the Ingram Pass road before descending the sharp switchbacks above Telluride. The section of road is known locally as "Interstate ½."

Ron Ruhoff Photographs

then processed under the large cam-driven hammers and amalgamation tables to retrieve the precious metals. A second cable tram carried the by-products to the valley floor from here.

Continuing down the road now, we head for Telluride. We have ahead, a series of nine extremely sharp, tight switchbacks to negotiate. Several require a back-up, since they are too sharp for a single turn. Be careful not to get your front bumper hooked onto the rear fender of your four-wheeler as you go down! Locally this road is affectionately called "Interstate ½" and if you're riding with an experienced driver, don't be surprised if he says something like, "You have nothing to worry about. This a four-wheel-drive vehicle and we keep all three wheels on the road at all times!"

Homer Reid used to enjoy taking visitors on these roads and told the story of a woman passenger who said, upon arriving at the bottom, "Heavens! That was scary. I kept my eyes closed all the way down!"

Homer, who was driving, said, "That's alright. So did I!"

On the third switchback down, we meet the branch road to the old power house and Bridal Veil Basin. In recent years, this road has been closed due to private mining property and the power house itself is off-limits to exploration. This beautiful castle-like structure, which still contains the old Westinghouse hydro-power generating equipment, was operated between 1905 and the early 1940s, supplying power to the nearby mines and the city of Telluride.

A few more relatively easy switchbacks and the valley floor is reached as we come out near the large Idarado Mill. The mill is closed these days, hopefully awaiting better times for the mining industry. A skeleton crew still maintains the property.

Now that we have completed what is considered the most notorious of all jeep passes, you may want to stop at one of the Telluride gift shops and buy yourself a bumper sticker which states, "I MADE IT OVER BLACK BEAR PASS TO TELLURIDE."

With this final journey, we come to the end of our San Juan jeepin' tour. I've covered the major passes and some of the most interesting side roads, but there are, of course, endless other roads to follow in this beautiful portion of Colorado. For further information on jeep rentals, guided tours and locally made maps of the area, I would suggest contacting the chambers of commerce in Lake City, Ouray, Silverton and Telluride.

An excellent historical account, with many photographs, of the San Juans, is found in another Sundance book, **An Empire of Silver** by Robert L. Brown.

Descending the most hair raising portion of the "Black Bear Road," Telluride can be seen far below.

If four-wheeling is new to you, I would highly recommend obtaining a free copy of the booklet, "4 WHEELING", available from most US Forest Service ranger stations. While there you can also purchase copies of the USFS maps for Uncompahgre, Rio Grande, Gunnison and San Juan National Forests for $1.00 each. These excellent, colorful maps have much information including most of the roads mentioned in this story. For greater detail, quad maps from the US Geological Survey are also recommended.

In closing, I feel a list of some of the ethics of four-wheeling should be listed.

1. Limit driving to established roads. Don't drive across alpine tundra, meadows or cut switchbacks.
2. Enjoy, but don't disturb historic structures in mines and ghost towns.
3. Leave rocks, flowers and wood in their natural place for others to enjoy.
4. Respect private property and obtain permission if necessary. Leave gates either open or closed—as you find them.
5. Please take trash out with you and keep a clean camp, making sure fires are out.
6. If winching is necessary, wrap a chain or nylon strap around trees first so they will not be destroyed with cable cuts.
7. Use common courtesy with other drivers and offer help to those who need it.

Good luck to you and I sincerely hope you enjoy jeepin' the San Juans!

Ron Ruhoff Photograph

Still descending the steep portion of the "Black Bear Road" above Telluride, the Idarado Mill, now inactive, can be seen in the distance.

Bridal Veil Falls, 370' high, is Colorado's highest waterfall, and a local attraction in the town of Telluride. Three Needles Peak rises above, and the old hydro-electric power plant can be seen perched atop the fall. Switchbacks of the "Black Bear Road" can also be seen in this view from a hillside above the Idarado Mill.